"Realize" is the word that best describes the psychedelic experience. This is because new properties emerge from one's old ideas. These properties are not perceived as new, though. Instead, they seem like formerly overlooked facets that have now been revealed. This is especially intriguing, as a person begins to understand how these ideas have been affecting their perceptions. In receiving new pieces of their puzzle, one begins to understand how their prior ideas fit with newly discovered ones and what kind of picture they are making. In other words, new dimensions of thought are realized, but the ideas are often not so foreign because human consciousness is brought into the experience. A psychedelic trip is astounding if considered solely as an alien experience, but it is absolutely ineffable when it is convincingly connected to reality.

The Subsequent Fate
Christian Meteor

The Patterns of Existence II: The Subsequent Fate

ISBN 13: 9781736966327

Copyright © 2022 Christian Meteor

All rights reserved. No part of this book may be reproduced in any form except for the purpose of brief reviews, without written permission of the author.

Uncharted worlds lie within the minds of humans. They are not like dreams but rather exist as realms outside of our immediate perception. Like an undiscovered continent, these places are not created by their explorers. Instead, they exist in hyperspace and are composed of bizarre creatures and scapes that are governed by different natural laws. The strange dichotomy, however, is that we exist in the midst of these worlds, like three-dimensional beings in a four-dimensional reality. These places are not alien, but are rather unperceived portions of our daily experience. So, as a mouse navigating a maze does not know it is in a laboratory; similarly, we humans exist in a happening that is much larger than our senses reveal. A biologically beneficial "lens" filters our perception of reality, allowing only the most vital information to permeate it.

The methods for revealing these places remain a cosmic riddle. We can carefully follow the techniques offered by a voyager for access to them and end up somewhere completely different. Because of this conundrum, those who have traveled to these places often create a representation of what it is like to be there, such as artwork or sacred geometry. These can be accurate portrayals of the experience, but full immersion is the only way to completely understand those places. However, the return to our reality often obscures much of what we saw and experienced, and therefore these representations can only partially capture the feeling, and expose a fraction of the broader happening.

The fact that this kind of art succeeds in eliciting mystical feelings in multitudes of people asserts the hypothesis that these uncharted worlds are not individual-independent. The realms explored by Aldous Huxley and Terence McKenna were not "created" by them, nor were those explored by Gautama Buddha or Dante Alighieri. Therefore, humans' wonder for art should not be attributed exclusively to its novelty and beauty, but also to our shared immersion in hyperdimensional space. So, the kaleidoscopic mosques of Iran are not majestic simply because of their symmetry and color, but also because they are a representation of a not immediately perceivable reality that we all exist in. Art can tap into our innate spiritual sense of hyperspace that is suppressed by our physicality.

    Art can also be trans-dimensional, meaning that the physical depictions of these realms by humans have the power to transport others to places in hyperspace. The word "transport" is somewhat misleading, however, as it implies physically traveling to a different space. Instead, our consciousness is moving into the invisible world around us. For example, we can visually immerse ourself in a mandala carpet and bring our consciousness to a new place while our body simply remains on the rug. Psychedelics can help to achieve this effect, but transport is entirely possible through other means as well.

    The art of the mandala is like a code, only operative because it occurs within a larger happening. Countless examples of trans-dimensional artwork have emerged from religions throughout the world. A common notion about religion is that the spiritual worlds described are separate from our own. A more compelling argument is that the practices of religion only work because they affect the greater happening. Why should our spiritual activities have absolutely any effect on something that is outside of our reality? It is far more plausible to conclude that our actions, art, and thoughts impact the reality around us in a way that is not immediately perceived. Then, the notion that ascetic practice, rituals, and prayer have an impact is more probable in the sense that they affect a layer of reality beyond our lens of perception.

There is plenty of evidence behind the theory of an unperceived happening surrounding the human experience—just consider the invisible wavelengths of light. However, the specific components of that happening are where we disagree. This is asserted even more so with the infinity hypothesis, as the notion of duality is fundamental to anything existing in the first place. Religion makes subjective conclusions about reality which can never be universal because the foundation of the thought is not static. Instead of basing explanations on traceable and repeatable truths, conclusions are made in the eye of the beholder. Therefore, exploring the hidden world surrounding us is like mapping a new continent, but we cross the line from awareness to creation when we make conclusions about how it connects to our reality. For example, there is a large difference between charting the terrain of the Amazon rainforest, and explaining how cutting it down is affecting the planet.

Science is an incredibly refreshing solution to this matter because it bases its explanations on objectively verifiable facets of the human experience. However, these particular worlds are not objective because our consciousnesses interpretation of them varies. This is not to say that these worlds are ever changing, but rather that our interpretation of them is. So, for example, where one person may see a giant serpent preying on a boat, another sees a friendly snake guiding the boat away from the rocks. This is again where the line between creation and observation occurs, as one person views this as judgment, but another sees it as divine guidance. Each person witnessed the "same" thing in hyperspace, yet each came to a vastly different conclusion. We need only to look briefly at historic religion to find extreme examples of this—i.e., the Aztec belief that their gods need blood to keep the sun moving across the sky. Many believed this, but undoubtedly there were critics who saw a different path to ensuring the survival of the Aztec empire.

Indeed, when some interpret these worlds in the same way as others, organized religion is born. Instead of explaining actions according to physical laws, religious leaders create their own interpretations of hyperspace. This is, in my opinion, a great injustice to these worlds because, instead of exploring them, people follow a collectivized interpretation. While doing so is easier than actually experiencing hyperspace, there is a great potential for misguidance because the sage who knows the way to eternal salvation and the actions that cause suffering has great power.

Finding the right guide is not so simple, however, because many claim to hold the keys. And what happens if they are wrong? Do we then subscribe to another belief system based on another's experience? Our own experience should be our own message, as basing the entirety of our actions on someone else's perception is like jumping off a bridge because your friends did.

I am not so bold as to claim that religion holds no truth about the unseen connections in our world, but I find great potential for pain and misunderstanding in such things. We can be brought to ruin trying to understand the inner workings of Karma—wracked with false attribution, cursed to walk the fine line of "good" while anguished in a life of rigidity and looming punishment. This particular assertion is made by Jesus in the New International Version's interpretation of the Bible in Matthew 7:14: "But small is the gate and narrow the road that leads to life, and only a few find it."

This verse is ascetic at its core, meaning that the one who deprives themself of certain pleasures and enriches their life with the "right" actions will be rewarded with eternal life. We have free will and are able to walk in whichever direction we choose but, unfortunately, the incorrect path leads to death. To make matters worse, ideas about the correct path are not agreed upon and have changed over the years.

The major attractions of Christianity are forgiveness and grace—specifically, the claim that we deserve damnation for walking the incorrect path but that Jesus' death was the ultimate payment for our mistakes. Therefore, we are no longer cursed to the grave as long as we repent of our wrongdoings and place the burden of them on the cross. This is at the core of Christianity: that no matter how terrible our sins are, as long as we admit that Jesus is the son of God and died for our sins, we are forgiven and saved.

This is a beautiful fact, and one that sets Christianity apart from other religions. Christianity is not a self-help movement but instead acknowledges our inability to rescue ourself through our own actions and our need for Jesus in order to be saved. A conundrum arises again, however, as Christians disagree on which actions require redemption. A prayer of forgiveness for known and unknown sins is the most all-encompassing, but as Paul says in Romans 7:7, "What shall we say, then? Is the law sinful? Certainly not! Nevertheless, I would not have known what sin was had it not been for the law. For I would not have known what coveting really was if the law had not said, "You shall not covet."

Therefore, we experience guilt, a sense of wrongdoing, and the need for forgiveness because God's law tells us which actions are wrong. But again, different people have different notions of wrong, and churches have conflicting interpretations of God's law. This passage insists that the law is holy and humans are sinful, and that what was formerly seen as unproblematic now brings death. That unproblematic thing, however, was always problematic—people just needed the law to see it (few things exemplify ignorance being bliss more than this passage).

The notion of free will is particularly hidden here because the punishment for sin is death. People choose the path of life by enslaving themselves to God's law, yet still fall short, so therefore, they need Jesus to forgive them for their steps outside God's path. The law we are supposed to follow, however, is not objectively traceable, which means that the consequence of breaking such a law is not either. Our experience is subjective at its core, so shouldn't our relationship with God be considered that way as well? Such an idea is great in theory, but one treads dangerously into the realm of false attribution and paranoia by doing so. Besides, who is to say that it is God telling us to give money to that homeless person? Maybe it is the devil, encouraging us to promote a destructive pattern of drug addiction in that person's life.

Paul puts God's law rather simply in Romans 8:5 & 9-10: "Those who live according to the flesh have their minds set on what the flesh desires; but those who live in accordance with the Spirit have their minds set on what the Spirit desires. You, however, are not in the realm of the flesh but are in the realm of the Spirit, if indeed the Spirit of God lives in you. And if anyone does not have the Spirit of Christ, they do not belong to Christ. But if Christ is in you, then even though your body is subject to death because of sin, the Spirit gives life because of righteousness."

This verse suggests that those who live purely to satisfy the desires of the physical body will continually pursue what it desires, and as such, face death. Paul claims that taking actions that affect the invisible reality around us is far more rewarding, and affirms it by saying that we are in the realm of the Spirit if God lives in us. So, if we set our minds on properly affecting the unperceived reality around us, we will not be punished. The actions we must take or not take, however, cannot be wholly subjective as setting our own standards means we could get the reward easily.

Once again, we return to the same problem: a universal truth for what sin is. An even bigger problem presents itself too, which is what Paul says in Romans 9:16-18: "It does not, therefore, depend on human desire or effort, but on God's mercy. For Scripture says to Pharaoh: "I raised you up for this very purpose, that I might display my power in you and that my name might be proclaimed in all the earth. Therefore God has mercy on whom he wants to have mercy, and he hardens whom he wants to harden."

So, even if we repent of our sins by proclaiming Jesus' sacrifice, God will still do with us what he pleases. Paul understands the visceral response to this claim, and goes on to soothe it in Romans 9:19-21 by saying: "One of you will say to me: "Then why does God still blame us? For who is able to resist his will?" But who are you, a human being, to talk back to God? "Shall what is formed say to the one who formed it, Why did you make me like this? Does not the potter have the right to make out of the same lump of clay some pottery for special purposes and some for common use?"

Whether we see ourselves as stardust or pieces of God, the truth of this statement remains—who are we to challenge what made us? And if there are unperceived consequences of our actions, it is in our best interest to try to do those things that will benefit, not harm us. However, no person who provides such guidance is without their own take on it. Therefore, we are still adhering to another's idea of what must be done to attain "ideal" hyperdimensional input and thus are not making choices based on our own experience. Besides, even if we were making choices based on our own hyperspace travels, the very existence of these realms is based on the fact that our biologically beneficial perspective is not all-encompassing, and thus we can never fully understand the impact of our actions on hyperspace.

A feeling of shock naturally comes from this realization. In summary, we are asked to make choices to affect hyperspace that are based on another's perception, or, on our own perception, but in both circumstances, the consequences can never be fully perceived because of our limited senses. And, even if we do make the right choices, our fate ultimately remains in hands of the Creator. But, we're told if we get it wrong, we're going to miss out on eternal salvation, unless we do what Paul says in Romans 10:9: "If you declare with your mouth, 'Jesus is Lord,' and believe in your heart that God raised him from the dead, you will be saved."

We can be a believer in science, a major critic of ascetic religious practice, and even maintain that the entire intention of religion is to manipulate the masses, and still receive grace by this simple declaration. The salvation of evil people and those who consciously choose to disobey God's word adds another layer of complexity to the notion of Jesus' unconditional forgiveness, but again, the full scope of the impact of our actions remains to be seen. The real problem I have is with the idea of God's punishment or reward for those who take certain actions. To reiterate what Paul says in Romans 9:16: "It does not, therefore, depend on human desire or effort, but on God's mercy."

What right does anyone have to declare that their blessings or curses are a result of their actions when such consequences cannot be traced? The notion of a God whose hand moves because he wills it is far more compatible with the idea of "is-ness." For example, how much greater God seems as the one who gives blessings unconditionally. Then, I give thanks, not because I have earned payment, but because God willed it. Similarly, a curse that befalls me comes not from punishment for my past transgressions (or past lives, as Karma would dictate) but simply because it is. I have rest in death because I have accepted Jesus into my life and choose to be a kind person on the grounds of what I can immediately perceive the consequences of. Being kind makes myself and the people around me happy, and hopefully such kindness is passed on. Whether or not these acts are chucked into heaven to be redeemed later is beside the point. I make my choices based on what I believe to be the consequences. Perhaps, instead of the hyperdimensional effects of my choices, God acts in the world I can perceive.

All in all, salvation is guaranteed with a belief in Jesus. The real key is making a positive difference in this world and, at the end, imagining the story of our life read back to us, not because we will be punished for it, but because it's what we did in this life before moving on to the next life.

***

The purpose of this foreword is to eliminate any confusion surrounding this text's suggestions about Karma, God, and religion. Before we can venture to the realms outside of immediate human perception, a firm assertion of disconnectedness must be made. Mixing the concepts of hyperspace with our world is dangerous because it is a partiality, and thus the consequences may be unexpected. To reiterate, I am not claiming that there is nothing of value in such worlds, but that we must be very careful with what we bring back. Psychonauts may certainly realize lessons for life or other tangible things from exploring these realms, but I am an advocate of charting these places and sharing individual interpretation rather than deciding universal laws.

The very nature of human consciousness is subjective, and so it should be respected and reflected upon before any conclusions are made. The worlds that consciousness goes to rarely behave by the laws of science, and thus can hardly be empirically validated or disproven. For this reason, individuals experimenting with altered states should not only recognize the distinction between "here" and "there," but also take care of the tangible "here" so that the "there" can be experienced more purely. Once again, however, keeping these two realms separate is immensely difficult as they seem (and probably are) linked in many ways.

Despite my criticisms of religion, I do believe that it has great value and can aid people in their spiritual practice. I think that a person so bold to chalk all of religion and extra-human experiences up to "fragile minds soothing their mortality" is horribly disconnected and myopic. For example, a psychedelic experience is as real to the tripper as a slap in the face, so to invalidate it simply on the grounds of "not objectively verifiable" is like declaring the mental anguish of a victim of abuse untrue because they lack verifiable proof of their pain. At the very least, religious practitioners and consciousness explorers should be afforded the right to experience hyperspace and share their interpretations of it.

Any philosophy, whether it comes from psychedelia or a college classroom, must be tirelessly contemplated and have its implications considered from a diverse set of perspectives before it can be considered for implementation. Many psychonauts and religious people ignore this requirement when considering theories for their own lives, so even though we must base our choices on our own experience, a hasty implementation of radical philosophy often leads to unexpected consequences. This is exactly what I did—I aligned myself with philosophies gained from my psychedelic experiences without thoroughly considering their implications. This caused me an unnecessary rollercoaster of emotions and radical ideological shifts that are revealed in the stories that follow.

Chapter 1

Dangerous

I had just enjoyed a smoke session at Dakota's place—one of those special times when the weed hit just right. It had been a while since I had had this kind of high, so I savored the experience that I wished would happen more often. I could not find anything to assure this kind of high—it would just be perfect for no apparent reason. The same applied to dreadful experiences with weed, and so I basked in the fleeting euphoria. Dakota's vape was hitting just right too—3 mg blue-razz liquid, drizzled over tiny coils that were threaded with Japanese cotton. This, and the purple alien dabs, made my body feel like it was floating in warm fuzz, while my mind bobbed down a fantasy river.

It must have been midnight as I was enjoying lo-fi music before it occurred to me that I would have to drive home. What a shame—it was the first time in months that I had hit the jackpot on weed roulette, and the night had to end prematurely. Dakota said I could stay, or maybe sober up a little, but I had to get home. This was partly an unwillingness on my part to compromise on sleeping conditions, but ultimately it was my ego that drove me out the door. There was something about spending the night at Dakota's that I did not want to admit to my girlfriend. Certainly, she would have encouraged me to stay, but my subconscious desire to be reliable directed my actions.

2

I could drive just fine while stoned, and I had done it many times in the past. Plus, the way home was a straight-shot down a 25-mph road. So I said farewell to Dakota and packed all my weed and paraphernalia into the trunk before staring at it. I was violating the golden rule: break one law at a time. Drive high or drive with weed in the car, but don't do both—otherwise you're asking for it. I looked back to Dakota's now-shut door and wondered if I should go back and ask to stay. No, the drive was short and I had no desire to sleep there. I was going home tonight.

I started the engine of my red Dodge Charger, and the thermometer read 0 degrees Fahrenheit. The roads were definitely going to be icy, and with the drive home going through East, slow and steady was the mission. Their police force was notorious for giving people a hard time. Plus, Bo had been busted with weed there just a few months prior and was now on probation. Staying safe from them was simple, though: just drive normal and act like any other motorist on the road.

Two miles of straight road sprinkled with stop signs; this was the gauntlet of the drive. My mind tangoed with it a bit, but I kept my focus on the road and made sure to cruise safely. Only once I had made it to the blinking yellow light where I would turn left into the gauntlet did my heart start thumping. Halfway into my turn, I noticed an SUV with familiar headlights oncoming, so I pumped the gas to get out of the way. This was the only other car on the road that night. What are the odds it was a cop? Weed had a very funny way of distorting headlights at night to make them all look like the ones on police cruisers, so I usually assumed I was just paranoid.

Instead of going straight, the car took a hard right after me, and then I saw a white stripe with letters down the side of it. At that moment, I knew for sure it was a cop and that the familiar headlights were not a hallucination.

I could hear my heart in my ears. Would the cop be pulling me over for zooming off at the intersection? I had only done so to get out of his way—there was nothing illegal about it. His flashers were not on, but I bet I made him suspicious when I went off that fast. Deep breath, eyes on the road. Don't give him a reason to pull you over. Speed limit is 25, I'll hover right below it. No swerving or erratic maneuvers, just a boring driver trying to get home. There's the first stop sign; he absolutely knows that I know he's behind me. Complete stop, waiting a second or two to make sure he sees it. Now I have to pull off; sitting too long would be suspicious. Nice and easy now, we're doing it. One more stop sign and I can already see the light at the end of the road, the edge of his jurisdiction. Freedom lies just on the horizon. But wait, my plates are expired. There's no way he's going to follow a big red car like this and not run its plates.

Red and blue. I don't even think I heard the siren. I stopped immediately and breathed slowly. Okay, I have to gather my composure. He's gonna sniff out any fear and build on it to implicate me in a crime. For all he knows, I have done nothing wrong. Kill the engine, roll down the window, grab the license and papers. Thank God, everything's there. I held it all in my hands up on the dash, and then I heard footsteps approaching the car. I was almost shaking, but I sat up straight to conceal my face in the black interior. A few choice words would get me out of this without a DUI.

All I could see was his chest before I heard, "I pulled you over because your plates are expired." I was prepared, though.

"Yes, I received a citation two days ago, indicating that I have ten days to take care of it," I said, handing him the ticket. This surprised him, and then he started laying on the questions.

"Where are you coming from?"

"Friend's house."

"Where does he live?"

"Creek Apartments."

"Where are you going?"

"Home."

He then asked a question that caught me entirely off guard. One I hadn't prepared for, one that would leave me with an unsettled feeling within.

"Why haven't you gotten your plates renewed yet?"

"I was unaware that I had to. I took the license plate from my deceased grandmother's car." A potential checkmate. I didn't like using the death of a loved one to my advantage, but this was entirely true. I didn't know when I needed to have the plate renewed.

"It's your responsibility to take of these things," he said, unsatisfied with my answer.

"The ticket said I had 10 days?"

"Yes, but why didn't you take care of it?" There was a slight pause. I hadn't come up with an excuse. I drew a blank. I thought the ticket indicating that I had ten days would be enough. Then I thought back to what I had done that day.

"I was with my grandparents. We were doing Christmas gifts late." This sounded so good at the time, but then I realized that I had just used the death of a grandparent as justification for expired plates. This story was entirely true, but would he believe it?

The cop asked one final question, and I, of course, lied through my teeth.

"You don't have anything in the car that's illegal, correct?"

"Absolutely not, officer." He then took my information and went back to his car. I had made it past the initial interrogation, and I only had to put on one more performance to escape a potential criminal sentence. One mistake, and I would undoubtedly be slapped with a number of charges: DUI, possession of marijuana and paraphernalia, intent to distribute because cops love to think they've dropped a big drug dealer, and probation. Fuck all of those charges. I am making it out of this. The time between the officer confronting me and returning to his vehicle was simply the "matinee" in my performance. A few minutes to prepare my next act.

    Once the officer returned, he said: "Alright, here's the deal, I'm not going to give you a ticket because you've already been cited." You're damn right you're not. Then, after lecturing me about "adulthood" and taking care of business, the cop handed back my information. He even complimented me on my car, but I was in no mood to chat. I was almost in the clear. Just a few more seconds and I would be home free! "Now take care of this as soon as possible."

    "Yes, sir." Then, in a split second, I saw him lean his fat, pink face down and peek into my car. We locked eyes, but the shroud of darkness kept me safe. This was the moment that could have spoiled it all. The moment when he sees my low, red eyes, and realized that he has just been played by a stoned kid that managed to get out of a DUI with word play. But, to my great relief, he stood back up and returned to his vehicle. Success.

    I waited for a moment before shifting into drive, slowly creeping off to the next stop sign. He followed. I would be out of his jurisdiction in the next mile. I drove straight down the road and watched as he turned off. Part of me felt an urge to lay on the horn. To smash the accelerator and rip down the last stretch of road. The sound of a V8 engine tearing off into the distance would be the last that cop ever heard of me. But I fought the urge. I valued my safety and wanted no more grief from the man. I drove home slowly, instinctively slowing down at flashing yellows and keeping my eyes fixed on the road. I imagined what it would be like if another cop ran my plates and I had to go through the whole ordeal again. Thankfully, instead of another psychologically jarring encounter with the police, I made it home safely.

8

Chapter 2

ABV

I was on the way to a lakeshore festival, coming up on a heavy dose of weed edibles with Louis. Heub was our designated driver, and the plan was to swim before we took the boardwalk into the city for food and games. A hot summer day with no obligations and a big lake to cool off in would pair perfectly with a strong high. I could not remember the last time I had taken edibles, and Louis hatched a great plan for dosing up: "ABV." This was weed that had "already been vaped," and thus decarboxylated so you could eat it and get effects. So that's what we did—we threw a few grams on our peanut butter sandwiches and chowed down.

We made it to the beach around 5 pm but had to drive another half mile just to find parking. The weather was really muggy, and I knew that walking back to the car covered in wet sand and sweat would be miserable, but swimming in the lake was worth it. We trekked all the way to the beach on a narrow sidewalk with cars whipping by, and I was thankful when we arrived unscathed. Weed never made me so high that I ignored traffic; rather, I hyper-focused on staying safe. Consequently, I would find myself disconnected from everything else and have to purposefully shift my focus to attend to them. For example, walking up the curb required me to look down at my feet and carefully avoid gashing my big toe. What a terrible thing that would be to have at the beach; grains of sand embedding themselves in my flesh and a pervasive stinging as the water flapped my skin like a flag. Just thinking about this made me tread carefully.

We had to wait in line at the changing rooms, and once I was alone in there, I felt detached. My mind was thoroughly distracted with accelerating thoughts, and I had to consciously go through all the actions of changing into my suit. The floor was also wet; whether it was urine or lake water, I did not know, but a nice glazing ended up on my feet and in my suit as I put it on. The beach changing room was always like this, but it felt particularly foul at this moment. The sound from outside was muffled, and the only thing I could hear was the hum of a big industrial fan. Being naked felt weird too; what if someone accidentally walked in?

I was relieved to exit that room and meet up with Louis outside.

"I was tripping in there, man. These edibles are hitting." He looked at me and nodded. "Are you feeling it yet? I'm really excited to swim!"

"Not as much as you are," he said, walking to the corner of the building.

"Where's Heub?" I asked.

"He's still getting changed. You were freaking out

that girl over there, by the way," Louis said, nodding over my shoulder.

"Who?"

I spun around and searched, but I quickly realized that would probably scare her even more, so I found a bench a ways away and sat down. Louis lingered for an uncomfortable moment before Heub finally came out, and then we all brought our towels down to the edge of the water. I was high and suggested that we wait a bit before jumping in, but just sitting on the beach felt weird, as if everyone were watching and asking why we were not swimming. This is what people do on the beach, though—sit and stare at the water. We were doing exactly what we were supposed to. Then a seagull came skittering across the beach and stopped to get a look at us. Louis and I stared back. This white bird was very defined. His edges were clear and his color popped against the blue and beige background.

"That bird is . . . crazy man," I said, still staring at it.

"I was just about to say that. He looks really cool," Louis affirmed. Another moment of silence passed before the two of us looked left to see Heub now standing up and looking at us with a grin.

"You guys are pretty stoned, aren't ya?"

I laughed, and Louis smiled. The whole negative energy of the changing room was gone, and now I felt ready to get in the water. I asked my friends if they were ready, and then we all walked to the edge of the lake. The tide crept gently up the shore as small waves pulsed back and forth. I started by dipping a toe into the gooey, wet sand. It was a little chilly but certainly swimmable for this time of year. I was hot, too, and decided that the next step was to get in. I started to wade with Louis, and as the water got to my knees, I watched him plunge all the way in with a look of sheer euphoria on his face. That was the right idea, and I was going to follow suit, but I wondered where Heub was. I looked back to see him still testing the water on shore; typical. I had waited long enough and plunged in. Water enveloped my body and cooled my core, but it felt as if my skin were protecting me from the cold piercing too deeply.

Then I emerged, breaking the surface like a dolphin savoring the day's first swim. It felt amazing, and I had to go again, so I plunged back in, feeling the water with all of my skin. Upon coming up, I felt gobs of water falling off my body, as if I were a sea monster bringing a flood. I was joyous, and I wondered if Louis was having as good a time as I was. I watched as he jumped in and out of the water like a dolphin, devoid of any self-consciousness or worry, fully immersed in the fun. This was exactly how to swim on edibles; pure bliss.

The picture of the shore that day is burned into my mind—crystal clear edges and saturated with color, like it was in high definition. Distant greenery speckled the sand dunes against a pure blue sky. I had gone to this beach my whole childhood, but today it looked like a new land. It was as if I had come upon the shores of Madagascar for the very first time, soaking in the glory.

We had been swimming for about an hour before the carnival food and trippiness of the city became alluring. Our plan was perfect: we'd walk around town blazed for a couple hours, ride roller coasters, and get some food before jumping back in the water to cool off. There is a kind of guilty pleasure in strutting around in public absolutely fried, and we even had some joints to smoke in the woods to keep the high going. I looked forward to revisiting the lake later and watching the sunset, but now the munchies were coming on and it was time to go to the festival.

We headed to the changing rooms, and it was then that I noticed a twinging pain in my knee. I chalked it up to the waves pushing me around and tried to ignore it while switching out of my suit, but then intense audible hallucinations grabbed my attention. The whirring of the fan sounded very loud, and was now blended with a pulsating sound that invaded my ears. Then I caught a glimpse of my reflection in the mirror—I was wearing a bucket hat with aviator sunglasses and felt uncomfortably close to the bizarre mental space Hunter S. Thompson described in Fear and Loathing. Even the mirror looked distorted, as if it were hanging from two ropes and pulling away from me into the wall. I was paranoid about looking high and wanted to check if my eyes were red, so I got up real close to the mirror and could not figure out why I was not seeing any color. This space was tripping me out. It felt like I was stuck in a jail-like limbo, in a moist, beige cube being tormented by a powerful fan.

I burst back into daylight, thankfully fully clothed, and was soon reminded of the bad trip that was out there too. The vibe felt desiccated, and something about the heat was making my head throb, and my knee was feeling no better. My friends were still getting changed, so I found a bench to sit on where I rubbed my leg. My breathing was labored, and a cracking sensation followed each full breath, coming from somewhere deep in my back. What the hell was going on? The pain in my knee was excruciating, and each gulp of air brought the feeling of cracking ribs. How was I going to walk for the next three hours?

My friends found me hunkered over and asked if I was ready to go to town. I told them I was not feeling well and that I did not think I could walk that far, and suggested we go back to the car. I felt like I was ruining the day, and began losing my sense of self as I watched the sandy sidewalk become overlaid with geometric patterns. My friends tried to figure out what was wrong, but I just told them that I was in pain. I said that all I wanted to do was to go home and lie down. The day was a bust. We headed back to the car.

I could not remember getting there, but entering the car brought some relief. I was still queasy, and the base of my skull ached, but I did not want the day to end so quickly. I thought I might be able to make it out of this feeling, so I told my friends to drive into town for the festival. Then a wave of nausea flooded over me and I felt the urge to throw up, so I told them to go somewhere for water and a barf bag. They decided on Taco Bell, so we started the journey across town, fighting traffic. I couldn't get comfortable. The stuffy environment of the car was unbearable, so I rolled down the window, only to be assaulted by the growling of motorcycles and noxious odors of gas. The vehicular emissions stung my nose and radiated pain through my head. I rolled the window back up, then down again—what kind of cruel joke was this?

My nausea was increasing. My friends told me to throw up out the window, but I could not imagine doing such a thing with all kinds of people watching. My tongue swelled and, after getting coated with saliva, directed a stinging slosh of vomit out of my mouth and into my towel. I hoped that would be all, but I feared more would come. We finally made it to Taco Bell, and my friends went in to get water and a barf bag. I waited in the car for awhile before deciding that it would be better to throw up in the bathroom.

I exited the car and stumbled my way to the door. Upon entering, the whole environment was quiet and still; everyone was looking at me. I could feel my bloodshot red eyes, and I made eye contact with one stranger who knew exactly what I was feeling. After standing in the doorway like a zombie for a few seconds, I found my way to the bathroom and kneeled in front of the toilet, ready to let it rip. Thank God for the employee who had cleaned the bathroom that day, but the setting was still so repulsive that I could not get myself to throw up. I slinked back to the lobby and found my friends and grumbled to them, "I'll be outside."

Sitting in the car was nauseating, so I plopped down next to it on the curb by some red wood chips, sun-scorched plants, and candy wrappers. This place was outlandish. It looked like some sort of urban desert. As I stared into the chips, a shrinking feeling came over me. The pieces of dyed wood seemed to create an expanse before me, and I felt like I was on another planet. Then I looked up to see my two friends walking towards the car, carrying bags of food. They helped me into my seat, and I drank some water, which failed to help. Then the punching nausea hit, and I told them I was going to throw up. They quickly passed me a brown-paper food bag, and I expelled two rounds of heavy puke into it before feeling a warm wetness all over my legs and realized that the bag had broken. The tan vomit had some familiar things in it: chunks of ABV, bread, and tiny bits of trail mix.

My friends passed me the other paper bag, which I threw up in profusely before it too burst all over the car. Finally, Heub went running back into the restaurant and grabbed me a plastic bag, which I threw up in another three times before collapsing onto the bench seat. Heub decided to call my mom as the situation worsened, and fortunately she was nearby. I began operating on my most basic survival skills at this point, and found relief when my mom showed up to drive me home. The car ride took an hour, but I quickly passed out as I lay in the back seat. Home came quickly, but it took a serious amount of persuasion to get inside. After stripping off all of my vomit-stained clothes, I stumbled my way into bed and fell into unconsciousness for three hours.

    I woke up around 1 am, trying to figure out if it was morning yet. I crept into the living room and spotted Louis completely passed out, sitting upright on the couch. Heub was a bit fidgety, and I asked him what was going on. It turned out he was being picked up, so I thanked him for his help earlier that day and walked gently back to bed, careful not to jostle my tender skull. Then a massive wave of hunger hit me, and I went to the kitchen and ate a bowl of cereal, yogurt, some honey, peanut butter, sunflower seeds, kale and spinach, blueberries, cheese and crackers, and I drank a bunch of apple juice. I drifted back off to sleep an hour later. The next morning I found Louis in the same position, having slept upright the entire night.

    The vomit was still in the car, so I had to clean it up in the afternoon sun the following day. It was baked into the carpet and cloth seats and reeked like sour bile mixed with the headachey smell of a car. Vacuuming it up and scrubbing it was disgusting. The odor never came out, and the car from that day on always had a tinge of caustic-smelling musk that would become overpowering on hot days. I had never thrown up in a car from drugs before, and I appreciated my mom picking me up and not becoming infuriated with me for ruining the interior of her car. It was certainly my responsibility, and I decided to never eat ABV again. In hindsight, it was a foolish decision to do so, but the duality and uniqueness of the experience still made me wonder. It had been such a delightful swim, and I had been so excited to indulge in an evening of fun after, but like a switch, the trip went south. Cannabis had never made me feel like the devil was pulling my soul out of my knee, or like I had cracked a rib and was puncturing a lung with each breath. I also could not imagine a more cliché and nasty setting to throw up in than the Taco Bell bathroom, and trying to contain the vomit in a sopping paper bag was poetry.

If I could have enjoyed that extremely high swim without the consequences, I would have been satisfied, but with how horrible the experience was that followed, the swim was all the more delightful.

Chapter 3

Christmas 2016

I woke up around noon on Christmas Eve, 2016, and had a hankering for some fun. I decided acid would be a good choice, so I dropped a half-tab a couple hours later and then spent most of the day with my mom. She was none the wiser as we went shopping and frolicked in the festivities. My consciousness was hardly shifted—I was mostly just energized with a slight saturation boost that was not very pronounced in the gray winter atmosphere. Things were good, though, and the holiday cheer made it feel like the purpose of the day was to simply enjoy it. Nothing is better than basking in the simple pleasure of being alive.

The enticing LSD fairy came around 9 pm, though, tempting me with a more magical experience. I was lying on the couch watching A Christmas Story with my mom and stepdad, feeling incredibly comfortable and happy. This was exactly the kind of mindset I wanted to be in for tripping, and I had not had this kind of family-holiday bliss in a long time. The Christmas tree sat right next to me in glory, emanating vibrant, lustrous light. Everything was good, and I wanted to groove from the eve to the day, so I popped another tab on my tongue.

A minute had hardly passed before my heart began to race, making me remember the night of trauma I had experienced only a few months prior. I quickly took the tab off my tongue, soothing my mind with the idea that I was not yet committed. Most of it was already absorbed, though, and after a couple minutes of contemplating and remembering the good vibes, I popped it back in. I was ready, and this was going to be good, but would it be enough? I probably had a tolerance from taking it earlier in the day, and being underwhelmed on a night as good as this would be an injustice.

I tossed things over in my mind a few times and decided that I was going in—hearty immersion in the warm, psychedelic pool. With a tolerance, I would need a good dose, so I popped another tab and a half, putting me at around 200 μg total. I wouldn't be smoking any weed either, so I hoped to miss out on the raciness that had poisoned my last two experiences. This was a good dose, and I felt confident in my choice, so I lazed back into the couch and watched the movie.

The first thing that I noticed was a tremendous shift in my perspective on what I was watching. I had completely lost the story and did not recognize any of the characters. Everything was happening in the present. There was a marching band with a militant vibe, shiny old cars, and a strange middle-aged man aggressively talking to his family. The pictures on the screen seemed so foreign, yet were not-so-far-gone pieces of the society that I lived in. Then I remembered that I wasn't what I was watching and calmed down a bit. What a bizarre world it was that people lived in in the 50's. I sure was glad I wasn't one of those kids.

The movie had not ended before my stepdad left and my mom went to bed, leaving me with a lonely feeling. At this time, I realized that LSD was a drug meant to be shared, and not having anyone to talk about it with gave me the sensation of "a great experience and no one to tell." So, I decided to call my love and talk to her, not only for sharing's sake, but also because the come-up was hitting hard and my nerves were building. The seed of fear in me was very real, but talking to my love as the effects began to plateau kept me stable. She had staved off my panic on multiple occasions, reminding me that the notion of a predetermined system was incongruent with the idea of evolution.

The next two hours consisted of a back and forth between the two of us, unpacking the implications of natural selection and limited perception. Her words were crystal clear and truthful. They guided me out of the deceptive corridors of the acid realm. The notion that stuck so strongly with me was that of the human brain only being able to detect that which it was evolved to, implying that more awareness lay in the future. I internalized and sincerely believed this, which disproved the terrifying thought-loop of a robotic reality.

I would occasionally frustrate her, however, when I responded with something that appeared entirely off topic, seemingly ignorant of what she was sharing. I hated the idea of her words feeling unvalued, as they were the most precious thing to me, but I was having 10 different conversations with her in my mind at once. One about the visuals, the other about robots, another about systems, evolution, and consciousness. I had trouble keeping them straight, but her input on each conversation seemed perfectly connected to the next. These links became crystal clear to me, and were happening in seconds, so I shared with her how I saw them connecting. In doing so, I confused her, and had to take the time to explain how I got there from what she was saying.

I dearly wanted my love to stay on the phone with me. She wanted me to enjoy the visuals and the trip, but as the night drew on, she expressed her need for sleep. I did not want a repeat of the last time we had had a similar conversation, when I had kept her up all night, so I worked my mind towards what being alone would be like before finally saying a long goodbye. Then I was in it: LSD on Christmas Eve.

Finally, after two racey experiences, I had my feet settled in the trip, and it was time to go off on my own. The walls breathed and the room gently shrank and swelled, but looking at things head on seemed mostly normal. Only in my peripherals did the environment warp, especially the Christmas tree, which was transformed into a shimmering mosaic of festive colors. The skin on my hand, however, refused to behave, and pulsed from glossy and smooth to incredibly detailed and textured. Behind it, the large, beige-canvased Persian rug, detailed with crimsons, golds, and blues, exuded a gooey light into the whole room. It was very inviting and familiar, like a three-dimensional depiction of a cozy part of hyperspace. All of the lines on it were clear, and the shapes popped and glowed as if they were magnified.

The visuals were mild compared to what was happening in my mind. This was the first time I had enough mental stability in my trip to be conscious of how LSD was affecting my thoughts without getting me too drawn into them. Some proved incredibly enticing, but I knew that staying comfortably detached from my racing ideas was the best choice. This was not all pleasant, though, and I found myself a bit "sideways" with the hyper-thought connectivity because I didn't really have a choice in the matter. All my ideas were very intense, whether I liked it or not, so I had to proceed very cautiously with where my mind went, lest I be taken on a freaky train. I didn't have much distracting me from this either; I was just sitting on the couch feeling everything the acid was doing to my brain.

Then I remembered music: a glorious world of sound to get completely lost in. I grabbed my headphones and immediately put on "Break on Through" by The Doors. Every sound was much wider, drawn out, and distorted. This was pure creation expressed as an audible adventure made by a man tripping on LSD himself. His guitar plucks echoed and seemed to linger in sound space before fluidly connecting to the next note. Instead of my thoughts twisting at 100 mph, they were preoccupied only with the sound. My full immersion was almost uni-sensory, as if sound were the only perception that I was experiencing.

I had to keep it going, so I pulled up the band 1200 Micrograms and put on the song "LSD." This music had warbley tunes, like a sheet of galactic plastic being wiggled in a bright neon alien city, filled with pinks, lime-greens, oranges, and cyans. It was transportive, but not in a visual sense. Instead, I felt like I was in that kind of space.

I cycled through music for about an hour before the walls of my sanity began degrading again. I had been texting my love, telling her about the effects, and dealing with my racing thoughts on the reasons behind my texting difficulty. At first, I had decided that I was having difficulty texting her because the universe was seeing me as unfit and that I was undeserving. Then I remembered that I was a creature, an ape using meaty fingers to touch tiny keys on this cellular device. I made a beastly noise with this realization and then continued texting her, telling her how much I loved her.

This is how many of my thoughts would evolve throughout this trip. I would make assumptions about the reasons that things were happening to me, for good or bad, immediately upon them occurring. I did not do this consciously. The spark of any thought would result in pages and pages of inquiry on that subject, and within seconds, I would have a well-rounded conclusion. I could work through weeks of thoughts in a matter of minutes, and either be amazed at their cosmic beauty or terrified by their sinister implications.

I was about four hours into the trip when I decided that I wanted to watch a movie. My thoughts were spiraling a bit, and though I did not fear psychosis, the amount of mental work I was doing to keep myself sane was tiring. I put on Fear and Loathing in Las Vegas, a story I had watched and read countless times under the influence of many drugs. Each substance made it a bit different, and I knew the storyline so well that any weird emotional segments or shocking scenes were muted. It was still weird, sure, but just enough to seem normal on acid. Besides, I had already experienced the movie on mushrooms and marijuana; it was only fitting to see what it would be like on LSD.

The story, strangely, made sense like never before. Normally, watching this movie was amusing and perplexing because of its absurdity, but this time I actually understood what these guys were doing: speeding through the desert to check into a hotel to cover a race. Their urgency made sense to me, and though I saw the whole setting in a different light, I felt comfortably immersed. My mind could not watch the movie and debate the origins of my thoughts at the same time, so I became very relaxed in a detached sort of way.

In this semi-out-of-body state, I began reflecting on the past few hours of the trip. I realized my role as mediary between the dualities of my thought processes. This was as frightening as it was enlightening, as I realized how convincing both ends of these thoughts had been. And this was the case for all of my thoughts—each one had extreme left and extreme right implications, yet at the time I completely believed that one side was the "truest truth." Then, when my thoughts would go to the other side, that would be the most true, and the fear came when I would realize I had been entirely convinced moments ago of the other side.

I knew for sure that this was what the music video by Cage the Elephant, Come A Little Closer, was all about. Not only do all things exist in a duality, but also in many levels of realizational depth. So, by "coming a little closer," the origins of such thoughts and happenings are revealed. The awareness seems to come from a broadened perspective as well as from the witnessing of the extra dimensions of such things. But, even with this understanding, a concrete affirmation of truth is absent. The only thing that there really is is a broadened perspective of this slice of subjective reality that may only bring further questions and a sense of unknowing.

My love had described acid as increasing the overall amount of material present for all thoughts on a trip, and I found this especially true. My mind was tired, though—I had thought about more in the last few hours than I had in the entire past month, and something about watching this movie felt poetically "still." The time was past 5 am, though, and as it turned out, I was not the only one hearing the ramblings of Johnny Depp. My mom shouted at me to go to bed. I tried to argue, but it seemed futile, especially given the next day's Christmas party. I knew that I would not be able to sleep, and I worried about lying there and falling back into spiraling thoughts, but the emptiness was attractive.

I chose to listen to my mom, and after turning off the television, I brushed my teeth and got into bed. I shut my eyes, but my brain was still racing. Staring at the blackness felt good, though, and proved entertaining as some hypnagogic hallucinations commenced. These pictures were like tiny neon hieroglyphs against a black desert sky. They were not intense, just little blips of glowing color that lacked any fine edges.

I did not think sleep would be possible for another three hours, but the last time I read the clock was at 6 am. Then I was awake and it was 12:30 pm. I felt like I had time traveled, yet I had been conscious throughout the entirety of the 6 hours I was lying there. I could not tell if I had dreamed or hallucinated, but now it was time to get up. My body felt weak but also pleasantly heavy, like an indica buzz. I also felt pure. My mind was slow and calm, and I could not help but smile at my first acid trip that had not been plagued by dread.

Then I was in motion for the rest of the day, preparing for the family Christmas party. Once people arrived, I went into a bit of autopilot but was content to enjoy the festivities and food. I shared smiles and conversation with familiar people, all the while concealing the fact that I had been tripping just a few hours earlier in the very room where we were standing. My guilty pleasure was wearing a rainbow peace sign; it had been dangling from my neck since the beginning of the trip, and I found a special kind of satisfaction in being able to function "normally" after the psychedelic night.

Only once I was alone did everything come to a halt and the hangover set in. I was irritable and angry. Sounds were intrusive and the words of others were annoying. Instead of blaming what was wrong on my own actions, I scapegoated my love for it, which then created even larger problems. I amplified minor nuisances in my mind into things I demanded to be addressed. I decided that my path to feeling better was to figure out some of the problems I had with things my love had done. My actions and shortcomings led to problems that proved emotionally taxing, and ultimately resulted in the two of us needing to dedicate a large amount of time to recovering. Had I simply looked within and realized that my problems came from my mindset and actions, I could have solved them and become personally stronger. Instead, I placed the burden on my relationship and made an even larger mess.

Ultimately, we recovered and grew, but I realized that I could have avoided the problems entirely had I rested before drawing conclusions. The days following this trip should have been dedicated to respite so that I could clearly reflect on what happened as well as let my emotions stabilize. Planning to deprive myself of sleep and then participate in a socially draining event was unwise, but that said, another perspective is that you can't always plan the right time to do a psychedelic substance. Regardless, a psychonaut owes it to themself and their loved ones to meditate post-trip.

***

LSD really is a "place." The mind enters it, rather than being just impacted by it. The acid realm seems to perpetually exist, but is not always experienced. That said, it's not really "traveled to" but instead perceived of. It is astonishingly strange, yet familiar and sometimes sensical. The laws of nature do not cease in it, so a kind of liminal experience occurs as psychedelia blends with reality. It draws far too many parallels with sober consciousness to be entirely disregarded. It accentuates the potential of the mind and can be a volatile experience.

Organized society and stability appear incredibly attractive while in the depths of a scary trip, yet humans' universal capability for psychedelic experiences suggests willful sobriety. Essentially, hallucinogenic trips are not stigmatized because of their divine fun, but they are avoided because of their potential for terror. All humans seem spiritually complex and sourced from infinity while tripping, but the degree to which they are open to exploring that varies. In a way, this is unifying because we all share the same mortal form and the problems that come with it, so regardless of one's level of exploration, there is mutualism. Therefore, in the company of others, a psychonaut should not brag, but instead practice compassion, as not everyone is comfortable going beyond their daily consciousness.

30

Chapter 4

Slater's Birthday

I showed up at Slater's house for his 19th birthday at around 9 pm, and after walking in with him and Louis, I immediately felt anxious. I did not recognize half of the people there, and I had been expecting a laid-back night of smoking. Instead, everybody was drinking, and two fellows in particular gave me bad vibes. They were 250-lb college football players, each swooning with a bottle of Jack Daniels in their fist. There was another guy, too, who was less intimidating but still mysterious, wearing a cowboy hat and an intoxicated grin.

I did not think they were "bad" people, but with Slater's four roommates and three new rowdy drunkards, I was uncomfortable. The house was small, too, and the only area to gather was in the kitchen. The rest of the rooms were private and off of a single hallway, so I could not find a place to go. There wasn't just alcohol either—Slater's roommate, Ryan, and the man who had given me DMT before were both on a candy flip, mixing MDMA with LSD. I was probably the least concerned with these guys. They were caught in a deep conversation, and with Ryan carrying around a stick that he called his "magic staff," I wished them the best in fairy land. They were still vulnerable, though, and Slater had previously described to me Ryan's battle with mental illness and pharmaceutical abuse. The

DMT man seemed to be handling him well, though, and I was more preoccupied with the lumbering football players who kept shouting their opinions.

I eased up a bit once I had found a place to stand and chat with Louis. Then I saw an exposed penis in the doorway, followed by the husky belly of the cowboy-hat guy. He was grinning, revealing himself to the entire party and ready to receive praise, but then the football players erupted in shouts.

"What the fuck is wrong with you? Get out of here before I kick your ass!"

Murmurs of shock and confusion wafted through the party, but the absurdity continued as the guy objected to putting his clothes back on. I watched silently as the color of one of the football player's faces darkened from pink to red, and based on his sheer size, I wondered what part of the room would be safe if things got physical. Again, he threatened violence, stomping his foot and shaking the floor with a scary thud.

"Come and fight me then!" the cowboy guy said, putting his hands on his hips. All eyes watched the football player stomp forward before the nakedness seemed to stop him.

"I'm not gonna fight you naked! Just put your clothes back on!"

The party babbled in agreement, and then the guy

exposing himself disappeared from the doorway. I was confused about what had just happened and found Slater, who was angry and trying to be protective of his female roommate. I was holding a bong in my hand, too, wondering when I could smoke to mellow out and detach from this whole thing. Slater told me to smoke in the bathroom, so I went in there and began filling up the bong in the sink. Then I saw Slater shove the cowboy guy, now clothed, into the bathroom and slam the door. I looked at him with a mild frown and tired eyes before holding up the bong and asking if he wanted a hit.

"Nah, man, I'm too drunk for that right now."

I shrugged my shoulders and took a hit before setting it down on the bathroom sink. Then I began questioning this whole sitution—what the hell was going on? Our encounter would only be as awkward as I made it, so I just played it cool and asked the guy why he had just exposed himself to the whole party.

"Everyone seemed so uptight. I thought it would be a good idea," he said with a look of regret.

I stared at him for a moment and, realizing his level of intoxication, took pity on him. Here was a guy who was way too drunk to drive home, who had been excommunicated from the party after making a stupid choice. I talked through his actions with him for a few minutes and realized that he had made an impulsive decision that was rooted in good intentions. I did not want any more conflict at this party, especially with alcohol as a factor, so we talked until the guy agreed he was ready to say he was sorry. He left the bathroom and went into the kitchen, where I watched from the hallway as he made a sincere apology. It was not well received by the football players, but the others accepted it and seemed able to leave his actions in the past. Their unforgiveness isolated these two brutes, and I was quite happy when they decided to leave shortly afterwards.

With the threat of violence gone, I mellowed out a bit and slid into my high. Then, my mind began racing as the DMT man shared that he had some. He told me that now was not the time, though, as he was in the middle of a particularly complex acid conversation with Ryan. So, I decided to join Slater and Louis in the attic, Slater's "bedroom." I could not believe it was considered a liveable space, but it was a nice getaway and being there for awhile allowed me to clear my mind and digest the past hour.

Our time in the attic was short, though, because Slater and Louis wanted to get back downstairs and continue drinking. I did not want to be alone in the attic, so I followed them down to the kitchen, where they got into a conversation with Slater's other two roommates. I wasn't really included in it, and I ended up just hanging out by the window before the DMT man and Ryan appeared in the room with the cowboy-hat guy. Then the party split in two, as Slater's group decided to go back upstairs, seeming to still hold a grudge against the streaker. Oddly, I felt more welcome with the trippers than I did with my actual two friends, so I stayed downstairs with them.

Then, the vibe changed. The room got quiet and I was waiting. I had been told I could smoke DMT that night and wondered if I would be able to go deeper than the last time. I had pretty much forgotten about the other things that had happened that night, and the DMT guy picked up on this. He asked if I was ready, and I said yes, so he brought out a scale with some tweezers and a baggy of golden-colored crystals. Just as he was about to weigh out my dose, he held the tweezers up and said, "These look like they have been used for personal hygiene." I looked closely at them and spotted a curly black hair along with some specks of skin and oil. Then they were vaporized as he held a lighter to them and said, "That's better."

I shrugged and was glad I had a supplier who could spot such things while on a heavy dose of LSD and MDMA. He weighed out the crystals and then poured them into the pipe before asking me, "Where do you want to do it?" My eyes widened and my chest tightened. Now? It was already time?

"Not in here. Um, I still need a couple minutes. Where do you think I should do it?" I said, hoping to stall. I knew he wasn't going to force me; this was my choice. I just had not realized it would come so quickly. Just like the last time, it was all an idea up until this moment. I needed to settle my breathing, get some things straight in my head.

"Well, Ryan wants to, and we're going to do it in his room. Want to check it out?"

I nodded and followed the two of them into the bedroom, followed by the cowboy-hat guy. The room had a mellow darkness and some neon blacklight posters covering the walls, distorted by the changing colors of the ceiling light that shined green, red, purple, and yellow, painting the room with rainbow hues. I sat in a desk chair and took it all in for a minute before nodding to them and saying that the setting was good.

"You should probably have a seat on the bed so that you can lie back comfortably after smoking," the DMT guy offered. I nodded and then propped myself up on the cushy blue comforter and took some deep breaths. I was still not ready, but I did not sense any pressure or impatience from him. I had as much time as I needed to prepare.

"Are you going to try it too?" I asked, looking at the cowboy-hat guy who was sitting in a chair at the foot of the bed.

"No, just alcohol for me. I don't need more."

At that moment, he seemed to acknowledge the damage he had caused due to his alcohol consumption, as well as a fear of an intense drug experience. I did not blame him. Alcohol may have been a familiar and comfortable substance for him, and without knowing his back-story, I felt no need to press him. Whether his alcohol consumption was a way of coping with suffering or simply because he enjoyed the feeling of intoxication, I accepted his choice. My conservative upbringing could have caused me to rant to him about all the problems associated with alcohol and alcohol addiction. My infatuation with hallucinogens could have made me advertise their potential to kick an alcohol addiction, but none of that seemed necessary. We were just humans free to do as we pleased, with a sort of mutual understanding of "live and let live."

    I talked through my hesitancy with my new acquaintances, and after being affirmed that the experience would last only five minutes, I began approaching acceptance. They offered me some headphones, so I told them to put on Shpongle Falls. The music played for a second, and I confirmed that it was what I wanted. Then I knew it was time. I put the headset on and then they passed the pipe to me. I held it a few inches away from my lips, and then the DMT man ignited the lighter. I twisted the glass bulb filled with crystals back and forth until a trickle of vapor appeared. I inhaled slowly, taking a small hit.

    I held it in for about three seconds before exhaling and going in for the next one. Halfway into it, I pushed the pipe away and realized that the experience coming over me was huge. I did not want to go any further. I handed the pipe off and laid back, paying close attention to the music and how it was changing. It became wider by the second, growing to the point of being completely unrecognizable at the 30-second mark. It was too intense.

I ripped the headset off. Then the DMT man said, "You lost your listening device."

"I can't do it," I said, with fear in my heart.

I laid back down and shut my eyes and watched as mandalas of purple and pink pulsed through a green geometry. I knew I was in it. I opened my eyes to a ceiling that appeared 20 feet tall and overlaid with a stained glass mosaic pattern. The whole room seemed to be stretched out. The walls were pushed out, the ceiling seemed higher, and as I looked to my right at the DMT man, he looked like he was sitting far away. The vibe was ethereal and fluid, changing with the overhead lights to hues of purple and crimson to yellow and green. I did not feel like I was in Ryan's bedroom anymore, but instead in an otherworldly perception of space. The intensity was growing, too, and the room continued to grow larger and larger.

I shut my eyes again, and I saw the earth sitting in space. Then I began to think that I was leaving earth, and I was scared. I had so much to live for here, especially my love. I realized that I was blasting off, though, and then I had some clarity. I, Christian, am together here with my love on earth, but I am leaving. This did not mean that I had lost my love, but that I was going to a different space. I would return, but now it was time to go.

Though this realization reassured me, I was still afraid, and I chose to fight leaving. I knew I had not smoked so much DMT that my blast-off was inevitable, so

I tried to stay grounded. I decided that I would stay here in this reality and that now was not the time to leave. I could see the bridge to the other side, and though resisting it was frightening, being in limbo proved to be incredibly enlightening in terms of my ability to perceive the connections between both realities. I was witnessing the disintegration of my world and the unveiling of the next while not being fully immersed in either. I clung to the threads of reality while being barraged with mountains of divine understanding and information that inspired awe. I was only experiencing a glimpse of this, but I sat absolutely astounded at the power and vastness of what was before me.

I knew that part of my resistance was related to my environment, and I ran through how I had got to where I was many times. The drive, this house, the people—all building up to what felt like a launch in which I was the spaceship. It seemed un-poetic, like I should have savored all those moments leading up to this extra-human experience, but now I was in it. I could not help the small distrust I felt of the people around me, but that came more from an unknowing than any actual suspicion. All of these guys had positive vibes, but the cowboy guy kept grabbing my foot throughout the experience. When I looked at him, he would let go and smile at me. I did not sense a sinister intent, but only that he wanted me to remember that he was there. The DMT man was guiding me, as he was the one who had brought me into the experience. Ryan was an explorer like me.

All of these guys were spirits. They were explorers of consciousness, having been to the place I was in and fully aware of the day-to-day illusory reality. I felt a great sense of comradery because they knew what the DMT realm was like. They knew the ineffability I was experiencing, and were as much in awe of it as I was. Even the cowboy-hat guy, with his repeated grabbing of my foot, seemed to understand some of what I was experiencing. I realized that his use of alcohol was related to his perception of reality; perhaps he too was aware of the vastness of the DMT realm, and alcohol was his grounding mechanism.

As I was coming down, the DMT man handed me a stick and told me that it was my grounding tool. I gripped it in my hands and felt attached to it. This was how I would stay here. I felt like I was in good hands. I understood now why Ryan had been walking around with a staff that night: to keep himself calm during an intense candy flip. Then I began sharing what I had experienced, describing the power and amazement. The DMT man knew—they all knew. I said that it would completely change history if we could bring back what was there, and they agreed, describing it as an incredible amount of knowledge. That was the word—"knowledge." It was information so powerful it would change the world as we knew it. Again, I felt a connection with these guys. They, too, were aware of the power in DMT and were, like myself, pursuing ways of manifesting it.

I was vulnerable but in good company. Even though I did not know these guys well, I shared my emotions and let myself be open with these people I barely knew. I felt like I was connecting with them on a spiritual plane, and using words as a way to confirm our shared understanding. Though I did not expect to undergo such an experience with them, I was deeply grateful that they were there with me. I saw each of them in an unfiltered state, not affected by cultural norms or personal boundaries, but as pure beings of love. I told them I loved them, and they all said they loved me too, and at that moment, I became more open to sharing my feelings with people in general.

I was a bit shell-shocked as I reflected on the experience, particularly the memory of lying there for only five minutes, but seconds had felt like minutes. The room had seemed so alien too, and though I had not completely given in to fear, the limbo was by no means a "pleasant" state. I had been silently begging for it to end, especially in the moment in which my breath was labored, the room was yellow, and I had the feeling of being stuck in a classroom. The clock: I had stared at it for so many years of my life in the classroom. Every fiber of my being resisted going back to that childhood experience. Never again did I want to be there. I recalled specifically my kindergarten, where I had not yet learned how to read the clock, and all I could think about was going home. Anguish is what this thought brought, and as I contemplated why I was forced into such an experience, the illegality of DMT occurred to me.

Perhaps the young mind is closer to hyperspace, and must be de-conditioned to it.

Many memories of my childhood came forth during this trip. The most interesting thing was that they were crystal clear. Pictures of the playground, the school hallways, the nap room—I remembered them not as stories, but as actual experiences. I recalled vividly what it was like to be in those moments, rather than the perception of an adult reflecting on them. They felt like more than memories because I was really there. In undergoing this reflection (that only accounted for a sliver of the trip), I traced some of the evolution of my thought processes. Basically, I saw where my mind was and the thoughts I had years ago and how they were affecting my thoughts now. I also did not find any especially traumatizing experiences in my reflections, and I felt good about having explored my past. I would no longer be subject to the claims of those blaming my "problems" on childhood trauma, and my mind could no longer trick me into blaming my weaknesses on things that I had no power over.

***

It had only been a liminal glimpse, some kind of boundary state where the environment was not yet wholly alien. Watching the room transform from small and simple to massive and complex in a matter of seconds seemed significant to me. Why should things in "reality" have absolutely any properties in hyperspace? I could be persuaded into believing that the psychedelic experience is exclusively otherworldly (and arguably insignificant) if it lacked these dimensional links, but the feeling of a dissolving lens and expanding perception is far too compelling. They are, without a doubt, vectors of celestial consciousness that reveal a much greater happening than we experience in our reality.

So, as one's perception shrinks while coming back to consensus space, the strange characteristics of the environment slowly fade back to normalcy. This is not experienced as a loss, but as a kind of reduction of understanding. The environment returns to a more simple and familiar state, not because it has changed, but because one's perceptual capability has shrunk. This experience creates an overwhelming feeling of ineffability because the divine understanding that was so tangible moments before is now obfuscated by the comedown. The mere fact that humans are capable of experiencing this kind of consciousness is divinely inspiring by itself, but the most mystifying aspect is the hyperspace links to consensus space.

By the end of this DMT trip, the only thing that I was more sure of was the existence of an extremely complex happening outside of my perception. I was permanently convinced that I had experienced a form of consciousness before my life began, and would continue to do so after. The return to society was shell-shocking, but the vastness of the ethereal realm encouraged me to comprehend my already complex reality, and to use my new awareness to do so. That feeling, though fulfilling, was alienating. Society's perception of psychedelic users was negative, and I experienced this starkly when I met the DMT man later. He was smoking a cigarette, and appeared worn on the outside, yet he was in touch with the heavens and spiritually adept. He was a drug dealer, but also a kind hearted guide who had helped me through an intense trip. This was true for the others as well: Ryan was a convicted felon who had robbed a pharmacy at gunpoint, and the cowboy-hat guy was a severe alcoholic; yet I felt a connection to and love for all of them.

The rest of that night continued as strangely as it had started. Ryan smoked DMT and put on magical World of Warcraft music for his trip, and then I got to watch him go through a full breakthrough, three-hit experience. He relinquished control much more easily than I had, and his humble expression and trust while taking that last hit was extraordinary. I had great respect for his plunge into hyperspace, and observed him quietly while wondering what the next level was like. He came to quickly, a bit disoriented but unmistakably glowing, seeming comfortable in the friendly aura of the group. Then, each person seemed to sense the moment ending, and so the group split. I left the room along with the cowboy hat guy, leaving the other two trippers in the room to discuss acid and MDMA.

I lingered in the kitchen for a moment with this guy before asking if he wanted to come upstairs to visit Slater and the others. He said no, and I didn't blame him, so that was our farewell. I knew that I would probably never see him again, and so even with an unceremonious goodbye, there was a kind of sendoff. We would carry the memory of our interactions on this strange night into the future, and though we both knew it was the end, the memory was a kind of asset. I did not know how that memory would serve either of us, but we had experienced more than friendliness. A kind of compassion, understanding, and nonjudgmental love that was momentary, yet lasting with its implications.

    I went back upstairs where Slater and Louis were drinking beer and vaping, and they gave me a warm welcome. I felt more comfortable now that it was just the three of us, and we chatted about the night. I tried in vain to share what my DMT trip was like, and though they both seemed interested, we mostly just enjoyed intoxication and carelessness. I had hardly processed it myself anyway, and I figured the best thing to do was just savor the glowing after effects. I sparked up some weed too, and submerged into a blurry high with my friends. Then my consciousness began to fade, and I fell asleep on Slater's floor at around 5 am.

    Sleep seemed like a small blip in time when I woke up to the clock reading 10 am. I wasn't tired, and I had never been one to stick around very long the next morning anyway, especially after that time at Slater's grandparents' house where Heub got caught for oversleeping, so I gathered my few belongings and told half-conscious Slater that I was heading home. He murmured something, and I wished him a happy birthday before leaving him there, drugged out of his mind, lying on a sleeping bag tucked in the corner of an attic, surrounded by his artifacts: a box mod vaporizer, a plastic baggie with a dozen Xanax bars, empty beer cans, a resiny weed bowl, and Nutrigrain bar wrappers. I pitied him, but knew that he was there of his own doing, so I said goodbye and went downstairs to the empty kitchen.

The room was a bit different now with the silver daylight coming in through the window, and it brought me a positive feeling of eagerness. I was excited to go into the day and tell the story of this night for years to come, and now was the time to let it ferment in my memory. The energy in the kitchen lingered from the night before as I pictured those football players, the trippers, Slater and Louis, the scale with DMT, and then myself—watching it all happen like some kind of play. It was poetically chaotic.

I was ready to walk out the door to let the story end, but I could not find my one of my shoes. The only other place I had been was Ryan's room, and I remembered the cowboy-hat guy messing with my feet while I was tripping. I thought he might have taken my shoes off, but I had no idea what had actually happened to them, given the fact that I was on DMT.

I searched the kitchen and then went back upstairs to the attic before knocking on Ryan's door. My shoe had been sitting right outside his door, and I figured that he had thrown it there and probably missed the other one. I waited for a minute and got no response, so I knocked again and then heard an angry shout from inside.

"I need my shoe," I said loudly.

"Go away! It's not here!"

I shook my head and looked around for a second before deciding that it was time to leave. I opened the front door to a freshly snowed-over sidewalk, and after my first step saturated my sock, I hopped to the car. Of course, how else could the story end other than with me hopping on one foot through the snow to my red Dodge Charger? It was the only ending that made sense after a night of drunk nudity, belligerent football players, psychedelic euphoria, and rampant drug abuse.

Chapter 5

Cigars

The first cigar I had was from a pack of Red Cheyennes during my freshman year of high school. Dakota was able to buy them back before the age limit increased to 21, so he, Bo, and I walked around my old middle-school block puffing on them. I wasn't self aware enough to sense the effects of nicotine on my body, but the experience of smoking was unique and thoroughly enjoyable. I wanted to keep taking hits, but Dakota kept a healthy restriction on them.

I didn't smoke anything for a long time after that, spare the occasional hookah pen Dakota got before anyone in my high school had even heard of them. Only once Heub turned 18 did I really get to experience cigars. He, Bo, and my favorite thing to do was to pick up white owls and smoke them on our old middle school playground around midnight. It required trespassing and stealth, but was a supremely indulgent way of basking together in nostalgia and cherishment of these temporary times. With the future so unknown, the power behind those moments was unclear, but unmistakably there. Our middle-school lives served as a frame of reference here; they were moments to be reflected on and served as astounding pictures of how much time had passed. The act of stopping to smoke with the mentally maturing effect of nicotine allowed for the gravity of the past to reveal itself.

Though we rarely knew how to express it, we all understood significance of these smoke sessions. These were special times, but without being able to fully grasp the weight of our memories, all we could do was savor the moment and share what little we understood about a fading past. We knew that the future was coming on fast, too; our paths were heading in different directions, and though it seemed unreal, our friendship was bound for change. A decade of playdates that matured into hooliganism and drug use seemed impossible to break, but the reality of adulthood was now creeping in. As children, our hopes and dreams remained in small confines. We knew that, unless something massive were to happen, all of us would be at school the next day, home in the evening, and by most standards, we would still be together.

The same was not true for the future. Heub had committed to his university, and Bo's constant talk of wanting to move to Florida could become a reality. These were life changes that would be detrimental to our friendship in ways we couldn't understand. We knew the facts, but how we would be impacted by them was a mystery. Together, we faced an inevitable future sadness that's cause was known, but with effects that could only be revealed with time.

Our basking in these emotions was short lived. Sometimes we would wander around the playground for a thrill, but usually it was just one or two cigars before we were headed back home. These moments were wonderfully nostalgic, but none of us spent time worrying about them. We just followed with pranks, video games, or more smoking. We didn't dwell on the emotions because we didn't understand them, and for that reason, we spent the night together like any other, as friends celebrating life and freedom, ignorant of the sorrows that would be brought by the end of our childhood friendship.

Now, cigars primarily hold a place of nostalgia for me, paired with a purely intoxicating experience: mild detachment, a cloudy headspace without much emotion, and pleasant physical effects—that is what I can expect from a cigar. Maybe a creativity boost too, but nothing spectacular, just a partial suppression of the inhibitory pieces of the mind. Nicotine, or any substance for that matter, can masquerade as the source of this creativity, but that magic feeling comes from one's self. Though substances can reveal it, that enchanting place is as much a part of you as the stars are a part of the universe.

Nostalgia, almost like a drug itself, can be generative in the context of learning from the feelings attached to the past and revealing perspective on the present. The extent to which this yields benefit depends on the person, but doing so balances it with stagnation. Memories of the powerful emotions of such times can bring a longing to return to them. In this way, nostalgia is like an entire other world, drawing people in with rose-tinted images of the past.

Some become hopelessly lost in this world, on an endless pursuit of a feeling that will never come.

Weed is a great vector of this effect, as it not only distorts your perception of the past, but also accelerates your thoughts and immersion in this realm. This can be great to experience with friends as you journey with them into the past and savor the times once had. The treasures in these ventures, however, are fleeting by nature. You rarely find something to satiate the feeling of nostalgia as it persists despite repeated attempts. The problem is that there is no cure; experiences inevitably fade to the past. This is why the anguish of a stoner in the depths of nostalgia cannot be understated. Whether it is through cartoons, classic games, or old habits, the soul seeking what once was should be pitied. The only way out is by accepting these things as what they are: fleeting diamonds of the past. Pursuing their mystery is a never-ending venture, devoid of anything that will truly satisfy.

Attempts to relive nostalgic experiences are even more disheartening, as the pursuant often finds that the magic is gone. The change in the people present plays a huge role in this, but even more so does the underestimation of constants. The monotony of everyday life tends to make the experiencer comfortably hypnotized, so aspects that seem trivial at the time are overlooked. In reflection, however, these things grow in power. For example, you might not pay any attention to a big tree out front of your high school until you come back years after graduation to find that it's been cut down.

Even with environmental consistency, nostalgia trips still fail to satisfy because of the irreversible perceptual shifts in people. The fact is that the feeling can never be the same because one's perception is dynamic. To return to an exact state of mind from the past would require forgetting everything since then. Therefore, nostalgia can also be described as a longing for reduced perception with mystery around the edges. This became especially clear to me with marijuana, as the novel culture and strange effect profile were more interesting than the actual experience itself.

As masochistically fun as nostalgia is, intent is important when engaging it. I do not think there is a problem with doing things for "old time's sake" and in the spirit of fun, but this can be a rabbit hole. Exploring the magic of the past is undoubtedly valuable, but a seductive haze of wonder and seclusion surrounds it. Far be it for me to declare that there is nothing beneficial in this haze, as many of the treasures I have shared in this book are from it, but purpose is vital on these voyages. Without it, one can easily get lost, which not only brings feelings of regression, but also disservices the present.

Wandering aimlessly into the past is alluring, like a dissociative drug. The past is vast and mysterious, and detached from reality, but it will never compare to the experience of the present. The three methods for finding one's way out of nostalgia are future consideration, acceptance of change, and wisdom. First, the past is confined, but the future is limitless, so an entire ocean of discovery awaits. Second, by evaluating the past, one can see why things have changed and how vital that change is to the present. Finally, with the realization of the beauty of the past, wisdom helps us to cherish the moment and buffers against future nostalgia. Purposeful immersion, along with the choice to remember specific experiences, generates appreciation and gives the experiencer a fond moment to temporarily savor again.

Chapter 6

Another Monday Night

The fourth time I smoked DMT was the last—March 17, 2017. Louis and I had bought it from the very same guy who gave me my first hit months ago, along with a dozen tabs of void realm acid. This was also the only time I had smoked DMT alone, and decided that I was finally ready to "break through." Three hits is the usual mark, but the dose at which one experiences a breakthrough varies. Some members of the psychonaut community have a particular egoism surrounding what is considered a "true" breakthrough experience. I dealt with a fair number of accusations following this trip by those who believed that my experience had not met the appropriate criteria. That said, I think that any person stepping into another's trip to define it is vain. Our place as observers is not to judge, rather to offer insight based on our own understanding.

I began the evening by watching dozens of videos about other people's voyages through DMT land. This is a double-edged sword when it comes to psychedelics, as preparation is a technique for increasing the chances of a good trip, but it also seeds unconscious expectations and fears in the mind. I knew that I wanted to do it that night, though, and after some back and forth, I sat down with the pipe and said, "I'm going for it."

I ignited the lighter and slowed my breathing, but the burning sensation grew in my chest the closer I got to accepting the decision. The closest feeling to that burning is being brought up on one of those roller coasters that suddenly drops—an unruly excitement equally matched with fear and power. I released the button on the lighter, extinguishing the flame, and took a long look at the free base pipe. A hint of doubt jumped into my mind, but then I said confidently, "I'm going for it!"

I put on the song "Ayahuasca" by 1200 Micrograms and waited until the beat dropped before holding the lighter beneath the pipe and rotating the glass back and forth. Then a small trickle of vapor appeared. I took a long inhale, and the familiar stale scent of burnt plastic wafted through my sinuses and reminded my body that this was it. I held the puff in my lungs as long as I could before slowly exhaling, and then the room felt larger. I went back for another hit, taking a big draw off the pipe and then letting it out once more. My senses amplified as I felt the intensity of this molecule, and then I went in for the last hit. I finished all of the vapor in the pipe, and then carefully set it down before collapsing backwards and hitting my head on the wall behind my bed. I tried to pay no mind to that, and slid down to a comfortable position flat on my back, looking up at the ceiling.

I was immediately thrust into an intense visual experience, as if I were being pulled through the kaleidoscopic intestines of a hyperspace vessel. Purple tubes meshed with green geometric patterns warped in and out of my field of view, blended with spinning red prisms and lines. I was frightened by the colossal intensity, but quickly found a Buddhist quote in my mind: "Conscious breathing is my anchor." I focused on my breathing and kept repeating this in my mind, using it as the foundation of my peace. My mind was not gone, though. My thoughts were clear and the same voice of my daily life stayed with me. I was processing and talking myself through the trip, fully aware of everything that was happening. That did not change the cowering feeling in my chest, though, as I was fully committed to wherever this was going.

I said out loud, "God is on my side. God is with me. God is with me." Then I felt a presence enter the room, and I looked to the door where an ethereal stardust whispered its way in. "God is in this room," I said, confidently. I felt his arms of love wrap around me and warm me to the core. "God IS in this room!" I said again, in a soft, deep voice. His care was immense, and then I heard with my soul, not my ears, that he was here for me through this experience. He's got me; I'm safe.

I never felt him leave—only that the writhing knot of anxiety in my chest had been replaced by a calm, divine peace, like the glassy surface of a lake. Inhaling was blissful. The air felt like perfect healing through my body, and exhaling produced what felt like the moment just before sleep: a heaviness in the back half of my body, and a floatiness in the front. I was soothed with existential peace, but also firmly reminded of the power of thought. Throughout the trying part of the experience, I did not give in to fear. I relied on breathing and I kept my mental dialogue simple. I recognized the parallel between the state of mind in the experience and sobriety, both being affected by my internal dialogue. Everything is in what I tell myself, and God is forever with me.

Chapter 7

A Bike Ride and Ego Death

Louis and I had been talking about having an acid trip together for over a year. Our feelings of wonder were mutual, as was the anticipation of a profound experience. By this time, we had spent over a hundred hours together wandering the ganja realm, so our desire to venture further was only natural. I was holding us back, though, wary of going in unprepared and suffering a bad experience. That said, I had been holding onto a ten-strip of 140μg void realm acid for a few months now. We were both eager to trip, but my decision came suddenly on a clear summer-day bike ride. Louis and I were at our favorite smoke spot: a hidden prairie in Thousands Park. This area was elevated off the bike path and surrounded by dense foliage. It was private and serene, right next to a chunk of granite where we kept an orange lighter underneath. We had smoked with it on many merry occasions, so the day that it went empty, we hid it under the rock. Each time we came back, we would check to see if it was still there to reminisce on good times.

This spot was an hour's bike ride from my house, and today, Louis and I had brought a couple joints in preparation. Once we arrived, my endorphins were pumping from the cardio, and the tranquility of being in nature was intoxicating. Marijuana was the cherry on top, and as I stood there soaking in the day with Louis, he wondered aloud what this place would be like on acid. The thought of this was enchanting, and it grew to be ever more enticing as I stared out into the perfect landscape. Wheatgrass speckled with wildflowers danced against the pure blue sky, surrounded by the mass of green jungle that seemed to stretch as deep as the ocean. Imagining how LSD would augment the majesty of this place was mesmerizing, and then I knew I was ready.

    I told Louis that this was the best setting, and so we set a date: one week from today. We would drop in the morning and then start biking so that the effects would not start until we arrived. The plan was to bring some food and picnic supplies so that we could make it through the come up and get settled in the trip before biking back home. Louis reminded me that we could just hang out in the park until the effects had mellowed out and maybe even watch the sunset. This sounded perfect, so I spent the next week thinking about the trip and getting mentally prepared.

    Oz, Louis and I's high school friend who had immigrated to the United States from Sierra Leone, got wind of our plan and wanted in. He was another fellow I had enjoyed much time with in the cannabis haze, and with him having never tried acid, I was excited to bring him along. The plan was to have him and Louis spend the night at my apartment and then drop the following morning. That same evening, my love joined us. Her presence seemed to promote goodwill for all. She exuded stability and compassion mixed with confidence and practicality, and her love for me was a security that I could rely on. She gave strength to all of us, sharing her blessing for the coming experience.

Once the sun set, though, she knew as well as I that it was time for her to go home. I predicted that some sadness would come with her departure, but saying goodbye was leagues more difficult considering what we were planning for the next 24 hours. I did not want to be thrown for a loop and bring her into panic, but I knew that my feelings for her would be intensified and a factor in the trip. I was confident in us, though, and as I hugged her and my heart welled, I felt her love and knew that I would take it with me. Parting was still challenging, as it always was, but I was in the right place in my mind. I was ready to go back to my friends and begin the process.

When I got back home, Oz and Louis were smoking weed, but their vibe was a bit restless—the same as mine. We were all excited and trying to relax before sleep, but wonder and curiosity percolated throughout the room. I knew that this was as much a part of the experience as the actual undergoing of it, and I had come to appreciate this state of mind. The trip was the root of it, but fantasizing about the effects and basking in curiosity was almost as thrilling. The accelerating thoughts leading up to the start of the actual effects are unique in and of themselves, and so the state of mind brought into the trip is already analytical. The starkest example of this effect is the mind's questioning of whether the current thought stream is a product of excitement or the actual substance. Full immersion typically follows shortly thereafter, but at this point in my exploration, I wanted to keep my mind together so I would not be overcome by fear. This would allow me to lucidly perceive the effects.

The three of us got to bed around midnight, but I was kept awake until 2 am with buzzing thoughts. I was the first one to wake up the next morning, so I made some scrambled eggs with veggies and woke up each of my friends with a plate of food. They returned the favor by helping me clean up my apartment, doing dishes, tidying the space, and setting up a good trip environment. I loved it, and embraced their kindness. I was fully trusting of both of these guys, and saw them as the perfect tripping partners for the day. My only concern me was that Oz had been unable to sleep, and I thought this might stoke a bad first experience. He was unconcerned, though, and I chalked it up to a normal case of nerves before an LSD trip.

By 11 am, we had my whole apartment cleaned up, backpacks filled with snacks and water, and bikes set up, ready to ride. Louis dropped approximately 380μg, I took 280μg, and Oz took 140μg. Then we were off, riding through the city to Thousands Park.

***

The trip started for me shortly after the trail transformed from urban to natural. I first noticed the trees: they were tall, covered in dense foliage and draping vines that formed a canopy over the woods path. I had to focus on biking, but looking up at the blue sky through the branches felt profoundly tranquil. I especially took note of the sounds—gentle bird calls against the droning of bike tires. I loved that present moment paired with the wonder of what was to come. Then the colors started to glow. The forest was a sea of green, but the edges of plants and their organic color palettes stood out. I paid close attention, wanting to be conscious of the growing intensity of the effects as the come up ensued.

    I heard the insects join in on the harmony. Their sounds were enveloping, surrounding my head on all sides. This, and the wind in the trees, was music. I was so in tune with it, too, fully conscious of everything happening around me. I did wonder why I had not chosen a natural setting for more of my past experiences, but this only affirmed how right my decision felt now.

    The color-saturated landscape and sharp sounds were convincing, but as my mind began to warp, I knew I was in it. My thoughts were no longer separate pieces, but rather continual streams of internal dialogue. Ideas, and ideas about those ideas, compounded at a rate faster than the ride through the city here. I could not give in to this fully, though, as I had to continue processing the path and how to navigate it. This became critically clear as we reached a stop sign on the trail where cars traveled on a road crossing the path. I checked with my friends to ensure their safety before quickly pedaling across and continuing the journey.

We were a little over an hour into the trip when we made it to a high point that overlooked some big ponds and the park forest. This was a scenic spot for a break, so we took the opportunity to catch our breath and soak in some of the experience. Oz was, disappointingly, not having any effects yet, while Louis was happily coming up. I had no doubt that the LSD would kick in for Oz soon, and quietly hoped that he would be astounded when it did.

The effects really started to shine as I looked out at the open sky. The edges of the clouds were spiral-shaped and wispy, detailed with symmetrical fractal patterns. I loved it because this felt like one of the very few times on psychedelics when I could sit back and simply enjoy the powerful visuals. I did remember my love, though, and pulled out my phone to check in with her. Then strong emotions came over me, but I was conscious of them. Things were happy and good; I had no need to panic. I remembered all of my past experiences when I worked through tough things with her, and they always ended in our love feeling the truest and best. I desired her dearly, but given my circumstances, I would have to trust that she was with me even when I was not texting her. There was a trip before me, and I solemnly understood this when I saw the concrete behind my phone transform into a mass of fleur-de-lis patterns. I think my friends also sensed that I could lose myself grasping for love while texting on my phone, so they asked if I was ready to get back on my bike. I knew that this was the right choice, even though I would have to temporarily stop communication with my love, so I wished her the best and told her I loved her before packing away my phone in a safe place. Then I checked with my friends, who exuded excitement, and I was happy that we were in it together. We got back on our bikes and peddled eagerly into the trip.

The flowers came next. They were all around us. Yellows, purples, reds, and oranges, like gems in a sea of wheatgrass. They, along with the sunbaked prairie, smelled divine, and I knew that this was the perfect day to come out. I really gave in to the trip at this point. The world was so vibrantly saturated with color, and the euphoria of being a part of it was intoxicating. All of my thoughts were quite literally out of this world, and I rode to and fro along the path like a fool performing at a carnival. Louis was as immersed as I was, blissful and mesmerized by nature. I knew Oz had to be feeling at least something at this point, but what was most important to me was having fun and soaking up every single second of the day.

Every thought that I had was intense and rich in content. In a matter of seconds, one idea would have a book's worth of commentary formed from multiple points of view. These were explored to their deepest levels, and because of their profundity, I had an extreme desire to keep track of these conclusions and how I had reached them. I had no way of doing this, though, and knew that they would slip away like an exciting dream. This was just a part of LSD, and the best I could do was keep little mental notes that were representative of the entirety of the thought process that had led to them, hoping they would spark the memory.

I had been leading for most of the ride, and was pretty confident in where I was going. The path did look a bit strange, but because Louis and I had biked these trails dozens of times, we recognized many familiar landmarks. I did not have a set direction, though; I was biking aimlessly. The only real "destination" was Louis and my smoke spot in that meadow, but I could not remember how to get there. I figured we would visit that place later in the trip anyway, so I was mostly just sight-seeing. That was until I noticed Oz clearly fatigued and complaining about the heat. He also was not feeling the trippy effects yet, and seemed to need rest.

I knew this meant we had to start heading home because the park was still a 5-mile ride away. If the heat was already getting to Oz, making it all the way back would be a challenge, and I did not want his first experience with acid to go south. His exhaustion made me think about my own, so I came out of the psychedelic headspace for a moment and tuned into what my body was feeling. I was tired and hot too, so getting home was the plan. Louis was not showing fatigue himself, but the reality of our situation did dawn on me at this point. We were all on acid, tired and hot, with a lengthy ride ahead of us through the city to get home.

I led my friends along the path that I thought went home, growing less and less confident by the second. This way had seemed right just moments ago, but now it appeared completely foreign and definitely the wrong way. So I stopped and told them we needed to turn around. We biked a mile in the opposite direction before I most definitely knew that was not the right way either. Then Louis weighed in, and affirmed that were headed in the right direction. Perhaps we had not made it to the recognizable landmarks on that path yet, so I went with it and kept biking. Our choice seemed right until we came to a point where the path split four ways.

"We're in the middle of nowhere!" Oz shouted. I laughed, but he was right; I had never been to this part of the park before. It was low land, surrounded by dense green foliage, with a rusty oil pump wrapped in barbed wire nearby. I had the strangest feeling, like I had wound up in some part of the labyrinth from the Maze Runner movie, and was completely lost. This was incredibly disorienting and shattered any confidence I had in our surroundings. I looked around to see if I could spot anything familiar, and noticed some tall pine trees on a mountain of sand across the street. This was even more bizarre, as the only memory I had of them was outside of the trails on private property. Dread crept up my spine as I thought that we might be outside the park, but then in a split second of lucidity, I realized we were on the south side of the road. That meant we were definitely in the park, but at a part Louis and I had never been to.

Fortunately, there was a map of the trail system at this intersection, so we all gathered around it to try to figure out which way to go. There was no consensus. We could not figure out where we were standing in relation to the map, but it was abundantly obvious that taking the wrong way would add plenty of extra miles to the trip. This was the moment when Louis seemed to come out of fairyland and realize the seriousness of the situation. He picked a direction, but I knew if I was having trouble orienting myself with the warping map, he had to be as well. I argued against going the way he wanted to, but after considering that no way felt right, I figured I had no other choice.

The path he chose led us up steep inclines and declines, and now I was starting to panic. I felt like I was overheating, and all I wanted was to get home, which was so far away. Oz had also become a grave omen. He was riding in the back, and each time I checked to see if he was keeping up, a feeling of sweltering decay came over me. The sun beat down on his ebony skin, sending beads of sweat down his temple that framed an exhausted expression. He looked like he was fighting through molasses, standing up and pumping away at the pedals. We had to get out of here.

The way we were going seemed so wrong, and I kept stopping and jumping off my bike to tell my two friends that I thought we needed to turn back. Louis insisted that this was the right way, and I would take his convincing to heart for a few minutes before stopping and needing to figure it out again. I decided to call my love at this point. I told her that I was overheating and that we were lost, but she affirmed that the temperature was not high enough for that, and that the acid was making me think I was hotter than I was. Perhaps this was true, but it did not change how I felt. I needed to cool off and get home. She then suggested that we use our phones to find the way back. I had not even thought about that, so I wished her much love and quickly hung up to pull up the map. Louis did the same with his phone, but nothing about my screen was clear. The display was warped as if it had drops of water all over it, and the blue line directing us home was along the road, not the trail. I did not have the confidence to bike on a winding 45-mph road, nor did I even trust that my phone would bring me home. We had to stay on the trail.

    I called my mom to see if she could pick us up, but she told me she could not fit all of our bikes in her car. Then Louis chimed in to say he knew the way back. I did not trust him or his judgment, but his confidence overwhelmed me and seemed to convince my mom, so I reluctantly hung up and continued biking.

    My adrenaline was pumping heavily, and I sensed that the experience coming was huge. I was barely in control at this point. The possibility of passing out seemed real and I was losing touch with reality. My most basic instincts were taking over. Even more intoxicating was the woods, and as I looked into it, I felt my body recoil into a defensive and highly alert state. My eyes were wide open, and I sharply sensed everything around me. The primitive loop in my brain spiraled. I felt instinctual thought processes surge and ways of survival consume my mind and actions. I needed to get home—that was the most important thing—but it was so far away, and I was in the middle of nowhere.

I began to think that Louis wanted to stay in the park and continue the trip. I did not trust that his intent was to get us home, so I was suspicious of his navigational choices. Besides, he seemed immersed in fairyland, and content to stay there. This was the first time I had really distrusted Louis, which was strange. We had been friends for a few years, and with many experiences together, he seemed like the perfect tripping partner because I was comfortable around him, yet now I suspected he wanted to get us even more lost in the woods. I did not know if he understood just how tough a time I was having, but then he told me to stop and calm down for a minute. I did, reluctantly, wondering why we were wasting time, before he told me to step off the bike and take it all in.

I lifted my eyes to the dense summer jungle before us, and it looked absolutely ethereal. All of the plants were alive and being in this environment. I was lost, but this was their home. They breathed and moved together with intensity as one beautiful creation. I was enthralled, and felt my instincts come to the front of my consciousness and begin to take over. It was like nothing I had ever experienced, yet a part of me that was inherited and always there. This land was magical, but I knew being in it much longer would cause me to lose touch with reality and give into my primal side. Part of me deeply desired to lose myself in nature with Louis and Oz, but with the coming trip being massive,

I had to be home safe. I needed to survive, and doing so meant getting out of the heat, so either I would enter into the jungle and find shelter, or get home. I did not want to leave that enchanting moment of standing there with Louis, staring into the majesty of the woods, but I had to.

    A small seed of cherishing had planted itself in my mind: I was thankful that my friend had exercised enough mental fortitude to get me to appreciate that present moment. I held onto this, but now virtually all of my mental capacity was dedicated to getting home. Louis was leading, and I had to trust him, but nothing looked familiar. None of the trees, landmarks, or paths were recognizable, and I thought I was completely lost in a part of town I had never been to. The intensity of my thoughts grew by the second. With each realization came intensified visuals, as if what I was seeing was directly linked to the degree of understanding I had about my thought processes. Damask patterns covered everything from the sky to the path, trees and bushes. They were overlapped and mixed in everything I saw. The world had a permanent saturation boost, and I worked strenuously to keep myself from losing touch with reality. At this point, I was almost powerless to my instincts. They had taken over and were now directing all of my thoughts and motives. I felt like a tiger, vulnerable to the environment, trying to sense any threats, because I was in a compromised state. The only thing I felt like I was actually purposefully doing was biking.

Oz had been falling behind a bit, and though I was concerned about his safety, my disintegrating sanity was a priority. Louis was doing a good job of keeping track of both of us, but I still had no faith in his choice of direction. The woods just kept going on and on, and then the path transformed from black asphalt to a rusty-colored muddy texture that made me feel like I was in a rocky desert. This was even more disorienting until I looked up and felt a tsunami of relief wash over me as I saw a giant concrete highway overpass. I recognized it. It was the first thing that had looked even remotely familiar in the past hour, and it gave me immense hope. I started to come back to reality, and even found humor at the absurdity of feeling relieved upon seeing a giant concrete structure. Never before had I felt so relieved to see something like that—usually nature was what brought my heart relief.

The path did not hold its familiar appearance for long, and soon I was lost in acid-land again. I knew for sure that we were going the right way now, though, so I practiced faith and kept pumping my legs. We were biking through neighborhoods, and though my primitive instincts had settled a bit, I had to work fiercely to keep my mind aware of what I was doing. All the houses looked strange, and I pondered the fact that people inhabited them. I saw front porches, lawns, cars, and bits of junk lying around. It felt like I was an alien traveling past lower-life-form domiciles, and the vibes were hostile.

The world was bizarre and changing. Stoplights and buildings would morph as I looked away from them, to the point where it felt like I was somewhere completely different while standing still. This was the home stretch, though. We had made it to Wayne Avenue, which was a straight two-mile road that led back home. But it was no easy feat. There were at least a half dozen stoplights with hot and noxious cars whizzing by, and my mortality was abundantly clear as I waited for my turn to cross. I knew my spilled blood and fractured bones would be singed on the hot pavement if I were to neglect waiting my turn, so I stared at the red light and watched impatiently as motorists took their damn time through the intersection. If only they knew the impending doom I was experiencing.

Oz was at least a quarter mile back, trudging his way through the alien neighborhoods I had just been in. I was relieved to see he had made the turn onto Wayne, but I was too anxious to wait for him. Louis was staying with me, making sure I did not dart out in traffic or take a wrong turn, but he was also keeping an eye on Oz. The growing and receding familiarity of the environment was tormenting me, but what kept me going was the street signs. Wayne Avenue. I go straight down that. Don't let anything tell you otherwise. Straight down Wayne Avenue.

I arrived at red light after red light, huffing vehicular fumes and feeling my core temperature continue to rise. This was undoubtedly the hardest bike ride I had ever taken. I had to pay such close attention to the road while forcing my body to stop and go at the right time. I had to dedicate every ounce of mental fortitude to keeping myself in reality, and as the heat and exhaustion got to me, I began to think I was on the brink of death. I was going to die if I stayed out here too long, and these people were taking their sweet time cruising through the intersection.

Finally, I made it to the end of Wayne and knew exactly which way to go. I pumped as hard as I could up the hill towards home and, after ditching my bike, ran up the stairs into my apartment. My first thought was water, so I ran to the bathtub and sat down in it, holding my hands out in front of the spout. I turned it on and watched the water dribble through my hands until it became scorching hot. This was some kind of sinister joke—I was nearly passing out from heat stroke and I got blazing hot water. This did not help my panicked mental state, as a bleak lens was laid over my reality. I managed to get the water cold and splashed it on my face and head. This brought my core temperature down, but adrenaline was pumping hard through my body, and I still did not feel well. I was relieved to be home, but felt awful and could not figure out why.

By this time, Oz and Louis were back in my apartment and unwinding from the ride. I still felt like I was overheating, so I was standing in the shower fully clothed with the curtain open. Then I made eye contact with Oz, who could not resist laughing at me and I felt both embarrassed and a sense of Déjà vu. This was especially odd, as the circumstances were profoundly novel, but it felt so much like I had been there before. I tried to laugh it off, and seemed to sober up for a second, but I quickly returned to a negative headspace where I struggled to keep touch with reality. The bathroom was tripping me out, and I was wearing sopping wet clothes, so I went into my room and got changed before lying down on my bed.

My bleak emotional state continued to grow. It was not like the ones I had experienced on psychedelics before, where the fear of intensity was the root of the bad trip. This time, I felt a kind of resistance and a feeling of futility. My friends were quite concerned for me, but they respected my demands for privacy. When my mom came up to check on us, I shouted to her for help. She came in my room and sat on the edge of the bed. I walled off my emotions to her presence. I was fully preoccupied with the fear of dying, and I could not feel any love. I spiraled into doomed thought loop.

I was conscious of the fact that my friends were just a room away, though, so part of me was refusing to be vulnerable because of their presence. I was especially reminded of this when I heard Oz talking to my love on the phone, and asking her whether my behavior was normal. I felt jealousy and helplessness, as if I could not have her right now. I could not express that, though, because that seemed to my mother unhappy and she would threaten to leave if I shifted my focus from her. It was as if I had to choose between her and my love at that moment, so I could not text my love. I had to listen to my mother.

Then my mom asked if I wanted her to leave, to which I quickly replied "NO" and begged her to stay. She asked if she could come sit by me, and I said yes, so she moved closer. I took her hand and started to open myself up while fiercely fighting the impending ego-death experience. I felt her love, though, and it served as a relief from the doom that still plagued me. The whole room felt dry and cracked. The white paint on the windows looked decayed, and a stale, yellow tinge coated the walls. I saw the true nature of death in those moments: a stale, desiccated, emptiness. The whole room had that vibe to it, and even outside the window, a tent worm nest damaged the tree branches so rich in life. This was a representation of the duality of life and death, and I complained to my mother about it. She was speaking words of wisdom and clarity to me, but I kept pointing out the existence of death and my fear of it.

My mother acknowledged that my current state of fear was heavily attributed to my spiked adrenaline and surfacing instincts. She said that my preoccupation with death was a result of that experience, as my instincts protect me from death. I still fought the reality of death and decay, but she explained that it was the LSD that was causing me to do that. This, of course, did not change my realization of the reality of death, but instead gave me a lifeline back to sanity. I was still resisting her love and care for two reasons: I had fallen into a preconceived notion that she was goofy and not to be taken seriously. This was a stereotype that I had bought into. The second reason was the fact that my two friends were in the other room, laughing. I felt like I was being made fun of for needing to have my mom comfort me.

    I overcame both of these thought loops. I no longer saw my mom through the foolish lens, but rather with an admiration for her wisdom. I saw all that she had done for me throughout my life and the way she had raised and protected me. I saw her goofiness as a way of making situations lighthearted, but deep down, I knew she was immensely knowledgeable and kind. I connected with her in this moment like no other. I solemnly understood what it meant to be her son and to love her. It was unconditional care and support, no matter the circumstances. She is my mom, and I love her and will defend her no matter what anyone else thinks. I realized it did not matter what my friends thought; I am bound to her and a part of her, so absolutely nothing would change my love for her. I especially felt this connection because it was not something new, but rather something rekindled. It had been there my entire life. It had faded a bit in the past few years, but was now restored and embraced.

    I felt like a baby chimpanzee, holding onto my mother's arm, listening to her choice words of wisdom. Every part of this experience felt fundamental. I realized that I needed to have this sense of doom in order to ask for my mother's help. I had to make the decision to listen to her instead of the spiraling thoughts in my mind. My friends' laughter was necessary for me to choose not to care at all about what they thought of me and my mom. I had to choose my mom over everything else, and even making the decision to set down my phone and stop texting my love was necessary. I felt like I was undeserving of my girlfriend because I was immature. Then everything went dark.

All I saw was space, like a spirit with no physical form. Tiny stars began to appear from the blackness before a massive blast of golden fractals woven with galactic purple filled my entire experience. I was not seeing this, but rather I was this, and then I saw a kaleidoscopic, fetal human come forth.

I opened my eyes to my mom looking at me with love, holding my hand. I was at a loss for words in trying to describe what I had just witnessed, but felt I as if I could not give in to awe as it would disconnect me from my mother. Then I remembered something she had said to me many years ago: that I had been taken from her when I was born. This moment felt like it was the healing of that separation. I had been reborn, and now my mom was speaking words to me that were elemental to my being. It was as if I were a baby and she was explaining life to me, equipping me with the tools to live so that I could experience life to its fullest. I felt like I had missed out on or forgotten this, and saw it as absolutely indispensable. I also considered my two friends' experiences with their mothers—perhaps they had not missed out on their birth lectures. Now I understood why I had to be here, and afforded my friends compassion. Perhaps they knew that I had been missing this experience and even though they found it funny, they understood that I needed it.

I remained entirely in that moment with my mom, holding onto her and working through the process of returning to life. I felt as if I had been equipped with ancestral knowledge and the instincts that were fundamental to life. Her words rang true and strengthened me, but I feared leaving that moment. I was happy there in our small world together, but she expressed to me, without words, that I would need to go on my own soon. That was the point—to not only give me to life, but also to let me experience it for myself with the tools she had given me. I told her that I did not want her to go, and she reminded me that she was my mom and would always be there for me. Her eyes also told me that no matter where we went physically, our spirits would never cease to be linked, and thus we would always be connected. I also understood our eternality—the bodily vessels we inhabited and the realm of the spirit we originated from. This realization eliminated all my fear, and led to the sense that my mother was giving me over to my girlfriend. Now I had received what I was missing, and my mother expressed happiness in giving me freedom. That was her job, and she took joy in it, telling me that she was supportive of my relationship. Her eyes then told me it was time, and I understood and agreed. She reminded me that my friends were waiting, and I saw this as the perfect departure reason. I wished her the best, and then she left the apartment. Then I mustered my composure, and went out to see my friends for the rest of the trip.

My bedroom was only a few steps away from the living room, and when I entered, I saw Oz sitting at my desk chair and Louis on the couch. I only felt a bit embarrassed, but upon picking up on the vibe, that feeling was replaced with love and compassion. They were not judging me. Instead, they were concerned with my well-being, and I felt great comradery with both of them. They were a beneficial and entirely necessary part of the cathartic experience I had just undergone, and so I saw them as remarkably valuable. I was totally comfortable with my friends and myself, and now incredibly excited to experience acid without the fear. The visuals were intense, my mind was cosmically warped, and I was confidently venturing deep into the psychedelic realm with my two buddies. It was perfect.

    The first few minutes we were together ironed out any misunderstanding. I found a comfy place on the floor and felt happy to give Oz the chair that I always sat in. Then he put on some music from the computer, and the whole room felt and looked like it was tinged with rainbows. The sounds were echoed and harmonic, and made a "grooving" vibe. It was like a bouncy beat that we were all riding on, yet it surrounded us. It really felt like we were in the trip, and after only a few minutes, something happened that I did think was possible. Our consciousnesses became interwoven. It was like we all knew what each other was thinking. It felt like our consciousnesses were on the phone with each other in hyperspace, communicating seamlessly at a rapid rate. This was to the degree that our words were only a fraction of our shared understanding, and as this effect continued, our marvel grew.

We were deeply engaged in topics of philosophy, love, hate, and solving the problems of our globe. All of our discussions felt like they were meant to be happening. Our thoughts were progressing in ways that felt both predestined and novel, like some kind of hyperdimensional wavelength that we had all tuned in to and were following. Unfiltered communication of consciousness felt like the solution to humanity's problems. This was abundantly clear to us because we had no misunderstandings and the cultural, social, linguistic, and ego barriers were all absent. It was simply raw communication and understanding. This effect was even more pronounced in my perception of my friends. No longer was Louis simply a person, but he was a spiritual essence as well. His color was green and his vibe was organic. It was almost as if he were in a childlike state of mind, in a pure and unrestricted sense. This was especially awesome because his consciousness, or spirit, was familiar, as if I had interacted with and known the essence of Louis for a very long time.

Oz had the spirit of yellow and reminded me greatly of the sun. The fact that he had come from a continent across the ocean astounded me, but he also was familiar. Vast plains and a primordial vibe came from him, like somewhere or something I recognized and had been to long ago. I saw past all of my prior perceptions of my two friends, and now saw them as raw spirits. I knew they saw me that way as well. I felt like a reddish orange, exuding heat and sincerity. In a way, I felt like we were all on the primitive African plains. I was a lion, watching intently over my family to protect it. Oz had his own pride that he would protect fiercely as well, and Louis seemed more like a gorilla—the king of the jungle. We all respected one another and our mutual values of honor and family. We were loyal to our people, but we watched out for one another like brothers.

The fully immersive feeling of our collective experience and consciousness continued. The content of our discussion was rich and valuable, and though I had a strong desire to save it in my memory, the simple act of talking with my friends seemed to be a record in and of itself. It was as if our collective pursuit of understanding relied on each of us being present in the same stream of thought, so no one could linger on prior realizations. We were headed towards something, and the only thing that really mattered was getting everybody to the same depth of realization so that we could go deeper. Spending time trying to record or document the understanding for anyone other than us was wasteful because this experience was immensely valuable and fleeting.

This portion of the trip felt incredibly enveloping, as if I were in a new space with my two friends. We were still in my apartment, but the acid seemed to have dissolved a lens over our perceptions, revealing more of what we were already in. This served as a plausible explanation for the sense of familiarity, as this "level" was accessible by our consciousness, and we most certainly had been to it in the past.

There was no doubt, though, that we were only on a base camp of the psychedelic mountain. Even so, our connection and the magnitude of the experience was stunning, like nothing I had ever experienced before.

The way my friends kept me out of a bad headspace was phenomenal. It was as if they could detect when I would disconnect from the shared consciousness or withdraw into self, and they would bring me out of it. This notably happened with the contemplated of my relationship with my girlfriend, as my consideration of all the possibilities spiraled. Both of my friends affirmed me. They told me that they thought I was good for my girlfriend, and that we had much love to share and give one another. Their words rang true, and as I considered how I felt around her, the word that came to mind was "natural." I felt like I could be myself around her, and not only freely give love and compassion, but also be a good man. This feeling was like an emotional bedrock; something I could trust and fall back on. It also did not require me to contemplate it deeply. I had it, and it gave me peace, so I could explore consciousness and spend time with friends without being distracted by uncertainty.

The trip was powerfully positive for all of us, but there was a shared futility in describing what it was like. Our words seemed to capture the effects perfectly for one another, but these were often only small phrases that had tons of unspoken meaning. An accurate description of our experience that would make sense to a sober person was helplessly fleeting, so when Oz began to describe what it was like for him, I listened closely. This was his first trip after all, and any tangible description of the magnitude of this kind of experience was extremely valuable. He described it as each thought being a massive book, and as the mind is paging through that book and looking at all the possibilities and things to think about, another even bigger thought comes in before you can finish the initial one. The desire to remain on the previous thought is immense, but the new thought demands attention as it holds even more profound and important realizations.

This was exactly what it was like, and though I cherished and held onto this description, even more valuable was the content of our trip. I reflected in this moment; on the bike ride, ego death experience, and everything that had led up to where we were now. The visuals had been stunning, and the spectrum of effects brought on by acid were bizarre, but the headspace had been undeniably the most profound. I did not see this solely as LSD, though, but rather, what my brain did on LSD. As magical as the experience had been, it did not feel alien or useless—the realizations had were relevant to daily life. They were applicable and seemed to have the power to bring great benefit to myself and others. The most frustrating part was that I could neither remember them, nor save them. It was as if a scroll revealing the secrets of life were being shown to me, but I was forgetting the words seconds after reading them. "Words" is misleading, because the trip happens by raw understanding and thoughts not bound by linguistics; but the sincere yearning to save something persists.

Then Oz asked to play Grand Theft Auto Five, and though it seemed improper to do so on acid, I had no reason to say no. He hopped on the computer while I continued conversing with Louis, but then a profound sense of detachment came over me. The game took Oz's entire attention away and thus broke up our merging consciousnesses. I found this particularly revealing in terms of how technology breaks up human connection. This was sad, and served as a reason to spend less time on technology in sober life. Then, because we were detached, the feeling of loss really hit me. I looked to Louis for answers, but he did not have any; we were in the same boat, trying to hold on to the fading existential realizations. The simple act of trying to recall points from the trip brought mental haze. I could remember moments of sheer majesty, but not the thoughts that had led me there. There were only brief pictures, and though I would get excited while my mind tried to summarize them, it was nowhere near as amazing. Now I solemnly understood the meaning of "it's not about the destination, it's about the journey." The way in which I had gotten to realizations was what was valuable. The conclusions brought on by the trip were only as good as the thoughts that led up to them because then their origins could be traced. I could not remember why certain conclusions were so powerful, which questions they answered, or the depth to which they had been explored.

I had gone through hundreds of realizations and worked through a library of thoughts to get to them. Now, I had no way of recalling those things and nothing to show for it. It was devastating, but a fundamental part of the experience. I knew that even if I were to meticulously go back through and find some conclusions, the absence of commentary leading up to those conclusions would make them as unimportant to others as they would be to me. If only I could have saved all of the thoughts and put them into a book, then everyone could see why the realization was so profound and why it made perfect sense. Instead, most of that content is lost to the trip, and the fraction of it that I have left is unsatisfying because of how lackluster it is now compared to what it was then.

This powerful phenomenon of a "lost existential realization" was not new. Both of my friends seemed to come to terms with this fact better than I did, but with them sharing in the divine understanding, I felt solace. Yes, the magic may have been lost to the trip, but at least we had experienced it together, and thereby understood each other's feelings. It was like a galactic adventure we had embarked on together but had no tangible proof of—only a memory. Pieces of it faded with time, but the feeling would never go away. Even though I wanted something to bring out, infinitely more valuable was the shared experience with my friends that would never be forgotten.

Oz spent about an hour playing Grand Theft Auto before hopping off and rejoining Louis and me in the trip.

The comedown was abundantly clear now, though. Our minds were not nearly as intertwined as before, the visuals were mellowing out, and the room was starting to feel smaller. Everybody knew it, and desperate for the magic to come back, we decided to smoke some weed. It sounded fantastic in this moment—crisp and sweet bud with a musky aroma, packed up in a shiny bong. Smoking felt out-of-body-esque, like I was watching myself smoke instead of actually doing it. The effects were also starkly different than usual. Typically, cannabis would bring a cloudy headspace immediately after exhaling, followed by general intoxication and "mind floating." Instead, exhaling brought no immediate effects until five minutes in, when all the colors started to glow again. Once my two friends had taken their hits, there was an obvious uplift in the room, and then we were back in it.

The frequency we tuned into was not as high as where we had been, but our consciousnesses were definitely interwoven again. It felt so good to be back together, exploring ideas from a higher awareness and shared consciousness. The previous hour of disconnectedness seemed like a gentle reminder that this had to end, but that we still had a trip to enjoy. I was still following the communal thought-stream, but a piece of my mind was reflecting on and cherishing what the experience had been like. I could not stop thinking about how astounding the experience of perceiving my two friends as colorful spirits was, and I was very curious about what that meant. What space had we been in together, how old were we, and what kind of treasures did the spirit realm hold?

    I knew that I was not the only one pondering the majesty of the last few hours, and decided that putting on some music would both pacify the vibe and elevate the room. I put on The Doors, and the artful melodies mixed with the echoing guitar riffs enveloped my ears and made me feel like I was sailing out of a cosmic storm. This seemed like a good time to try to get some thoughts out, as my friends were simply chilling and enjoying the music, so I pulled up a document and tried to write. Hardly anything came out. My thoughts were moving too fast to allow me to stay on any one idea long enough to get any words out. By the time I had half a sentence, I was already four paragraphs into the idea, and found the commentary unnecessary to write as I was already on to the next realization. It was like I was solving an existential math problem in my head and putting down incomplete answers without showing my work. Again, I realized that this is just what LSD is like, and so the most important thing is not to grasp for something tangible thing to bring out of the trip, but rather to enjoy the moment. So I did, and attempted to lucidly perceive the effects. Notably, everything around me was moving, from the keys on the keyboard to the wood grain on the desk. This effect would only stop if I got up really close to the object. Even more bizarre was my vision. It was as if I were pulled back from everything, and that my field of view was increased. This seemed like an effect produced by my consciousness being more heightened than usual, like I had stepped back for a broader perception of space.

The visual effects were pronounced throughout the entirety of this experience. Objects were wiggly and fluid, with deeper properties. From the walls to the floor, they pulsed with fleur-de-lis patterns and woven symmetry with lines of bright neon pinks and purples. I had experienced visuals before, but never to the degree that my entire environment appeared to be composed of something of greater magnitude. Nothing around me appeared simple—everything in the acid realm seemed composed of multiple layers of pulsing information, yet were still "real" 3D objects. These visuals were also bound to my thoughts. As my ideas grew in intensity and complexity, the visuals would follow. I did not seem to be in "control" of these visuals though; they behaved as external independencies. I did, however, find the persistence of the fleur-de-lis patterns throughout the trip very peculiar, as well as the molecular structure of the acid molecule showing up in the oddest of places, such as Louis's forehead.

Our conversations were encapsulating and inescapable. Each idea had to be worked out and explored to its fullest extent. Sharing our mutual understanding and perceptions seemed vital. Without that, the trip would have lost a large part of its magic, and these profound ideas would not have been explored so deeply. The mere mention of a topic proved to be a rabbit hole. Absolutely everything was multidimensional, and the implications of exploring our thoughts almost always brought further discussion on the intricacies of their connections. This is why our conversations were so lengthy, as the root ideas were only the tip of the iceberg.

Approximately seven hours into the trip, everybody was hungry, so I made us some rice and beans. This hit the spot, and I took note of that for future trips. A meal this basic was perfect because it was easy to make, soft on the stomach, and entirely plant-based. The food also settled some of the uneasiness of the come down, and had a mild sobering effect. The vibe was still trippy, though, and our heavy consumption of weed was bringing a new dimension to the experience entirely. The acid headspace mixed with weed was more distant, as if I had been at the controls for the last seven hours, but now I was sitting back and flying on autopilot. The mental break was actually very nice, and as I observed the diminishing effects, I sincerely understood why psychedelic trips were called "trips": they are, quite literally, journeys through the mind. There are unexpected turns, scary corridors, and breathtaking scenery, but you are always moving and heading somewhere new. One of the most fascinating parts is observing where you have been, and how that connects to where you are now. The mental ponderance of a month-long adventure occurs in a matter of hours, and then you are at the tail end of it, awestruck at how much has happened.

I had a great appreciation for marijuana in these moments, and how it was padding the acid comedown. I felt a bit of restless at around the 10-hour point, but I think that was mostly physical—our bodies wanted to move. We decided to go for a walk, and although the effects were tapering off, my motor control was poor. I probably looked like a fool that had spent the entire day lost in a carnival, but nevertheless, the evening walk with my two friends was very pleasant. We ended up walking to a nearby urban park, which was small and enclosed, and boring compared to the jungle we had been in before. The duality made me appreciate nature that much more, and after lingering in the mild, summer night air for a few minutes, we walked back home.

Louis and I ended up playing some League of Legends once we got back, while Oz chilled and toked on more weed. Once I was in the game, I began to analyze my play and what my goal was. I saw the game through a completely different lens: I was considering the favorable and unfavorable consequences of my actions, as well as very minute intricacies and how they compounded. It felt as if I had overcome some mental barriers to improving my performance and was now operating on a completely different level than the rest of the players, spare Louis. This sparked an inspiration, as I considered how powerful acid could be for improving my performance. However, I knew if I were to trip again, there would be much bigger existential questions to address. Even so, I cherished this moment for revealing some of the secrets of high level play to me, and again acknowledged the powerful impact psychedelics can have on many areas of life.

We were done tripping right around midnight, and

after some heavy weed smoking and hearty reflection on the day, it was time for bed. We ended up sleeping for almost 11 hours, and the next day was like a glassy lake after a storm. My mind was empty and exhausted, but I was thoroughly satisfied and eager to go about life. My friends were in a joyously peaceful mood, and although our connection was now only a fraction of what it had been, I knew that I loved them. The experience we had shared was colossal in its power and majesty, and nothing would take that away. It was extraordinarily unique and something I had never experienced before. As a result, I now felt a connection with them like no other. Though I knew saying goodbye to them was inevitable, it still came with a sting. I knew that we would spend more time together in the future and reflect on this day for years, but our big adventure was over. It was time to return to the real world, and I wished my friends the best in carrying the gems from this experience into their daily lives, as I would into mine.

Once they were gone, I chatted with my mom for a long time about the trip, and though she expressed awe and excitement, there was no way she could know what it had been like. Still, it felt good to share with her, and I had not forgotten my mother and my restored connection. I got together with my girlfriend later, and told her all about the trip and my feeling of open-heartedness. We spent a wonderful evening together, and then when it was time for me to go it alone, I gave thanks to God for everything that had happened.

In the days following this trip, I found myself to be a more compassionate person. I felt more capable of having deep discussions with people. I especially noticed an ability to hold eye contact. I had struggled with this my entire life, and now felt the confidence to look people in the eye and connect with them. This came partially from my realization that people are incredible beings, operating on their own unique level of consciousness. This trip emphasized the power of connecting with others, and the importance of considering their thoughts, struggles, and feelings. I found myself leaving social situations feeling more confident because I had extensively explored myself. I could be fully honest because I knew why I felt the way I did about life, and thus could interact with others in a transparent manner.

My human connections and grasps for shared understanding were different after this trip because I had experienced them at a much greater level. The realization that humans are capable of extremely deep consciousness fusion stoked my desire for it. I had to tone this feeling back, however, because not all people are comfortable going to that level. That said, it gave me great hope for the future of human beings because I had discovered that seamless communication, devoid of linguistic and cultural barriers, was not only possible, but also very valuable. Psychedelics as catalysts of this effect are incredibly important, but ultimately, this realization emphasized the necessity of unfiltered communication. It is, perhaps, impossible to achieve total, seamless understanding between humans, but I believe that striving for it leads to love, compassion, unity, and progression.

Chapter 8

Halloween 2017: The End of Time

Three months after my 280μg LSD bike ride with Louis and Oz, I was drawn back to the bizarre molecule. Even though my experience had been spiritually fulfilling, it still provoked an infatuating curiosity. My cup of psychedelic desire had overflown during my last experience, but now I realized that the effects were coming from a vast place. I had yet to process the last trip, but there was much more to be explored. I was not finished drinking from my cup.

This was a peculiar time in my life. My dearest love was 100 miles away living the college life. I had moved into my first apartment after 18 years of living with my mom, and I was again taking college classes after dropping out the prior year. I was smoking weed every day, along with heavy nicotine vaping and caffeine abuse. I had the financial freedom to spend my time however I wished, and I was almost entirely carefree. The most important thing to me was my girlfriend. When everything with her was good, I indulged in blissful intoxication and prioritized exploring consciousness. I wanted tangible wisdom to bring back from my ventures. I lived carefree, and though I went through a lot of the motions of what I thought it meant to be an adult, the pursuit of psychedelia was my passion.

At this stage in my exploration, however, I was no stranger to the miserable side of psychedelics. I did identify mistakes I had made going into those trips, such as set and setting errors, but even with this clarity, I remained hesitant. I had broken the obvious rules of tripping like poor planning and mixing substances, but I had also overlooked details that I was unaware needed my attention. These came in the form of physical mishaps, such as neglecting to carefully organize my environment before a trip, or through psychological ways like "unsolved" concerns and fears. Facing these ideas is an expected part of the experience, as the user ventures to strange parts of the mind, but I had far more trouble with this than my peers. Most trips seemed to unveil a vitally important and formerly ignored part of my mind that demanded immediate attention. This often came in the form of subconscious fears about my romantic relationship, but seemed to have no boundaries in terms of what it would put up for grabs. Because of this, I was very cautious.

My curiosity was burning, though, and overrode my sense of self preservation and some red flags at times. It was hard to determine if my hesitancy was rooted in these factors, or was simply because I was plunging into something novel. I often preferred "mental exploration" before deciding to trip, so that I could find the true source of my anxiety. That way, I could determine if it was just pre-trip nerves, or something requiring more time and attention.

I found myself in this exact conundrum on Halloween. Louis and I had planned to drop acid that morning, but my nerves kept me from jumping in. Instead, we spent the day doing some grocery shopping and chores, chatting off and on about the possibility of a trip. He was eager to go ahead though, and we had been planning this day for a while, but I did not want to go in with an unsettled mind. Finally around 7pm, he pushed me on why I was not ready. I really did not know, but I wondered whether my uncertainty was rooted in my girlfriend, that is, the idea of losing her. Psychedelics were notorious for making me face my worst fear, and losing her was it.

Louis questioned this idea and offered reasons why I need not worry about such things. He emphasized the positivity and loving nature of my relationship, and I found his argument convincing and true. I had explored and ironed out almost all my doubts and worries by this point, but the act of verbally walking through loving affirmations was soothing to me. This conversation ultimately led us to the conclusion that we could neither change the past nor know the future, so the best we could do was live in the now and cherish what was.

With this thought exercise, I felt better. Something was still off, though, but I could not put my finger on it. I felt as if I had solved my mental apprehensions, so there was no "logical" reason for me to feel this way. I decided that instead of continuing the pondering, LSD could show me something more about these worries by unveiling the deeper reasons behind them and bring me to peace with my concerns.

We dropped at 7:18 pm while sitting in my 400-square-foot duplex apartment in the city that sat above my parents' house. I took 250μg, and Louis dropped a heavy dose of 420μg. These were void realm tabs from the strip we had used on the bike ride, so there was no doubt we were in for a wild night. Putting the tabs on felt good, like finally mustering the confidence to jump off a diving board. My nerves were very much still there, but they were quelled by the exhilaration.

Now we had to wait, and decided to pass the time by watching some professional League of Legends. I had recently gotten Louis into this video game and was obsessed with it myself. I figured an immersive and entertaining match would be perfect for the come up, so I pulled one up on Youtube to watch. I was both heavily invested and very skilled at this game, so I watched closely, comparing the actions of the pros to mine. I talked with Louis about why the pros were doing certain things, and how their actions were contributing to the overall goal. Many things were happening in the game, with different levels of complexity, but I understood this and how each thing connected to the chances of either team winning.

I had been staring at the screen, talking extensively with Louis about the outcome, until about 8 pm when I realized I did not understand what was happening anymore. I was not sure exactly when I had lost the game, but I knew I had just been staring at one character moving around on the screen for a while. My mind was definitely "there", but my thoughts had nothing to do with what I was watching. I looked at the screen that had been filled with consequential information, and now saw numbers and icons that had no relevance to me. The memory of what was happening in the game was not so old, but the point at which I stopped understanding was unclear. I was now watching something completely different.

I hit the pause button, mildly unsettled by the fact that I could not follow the once entertaining game anymore. I chuckled and spit out some air before saying, "I have no idea what's going on."

"Oh, it's just been swirling colors for the last 15 minutes for me," Louis said, unsurprised. I laughed and looked back at the screen with a smile before saying, "It's begun."

I figured there was not much more we could get out of watching the game, so I turned my attention to Louis and asked him about his effects. He described an oncoming visual experience, along with thought disorganization and some confusion. This, and his wide-eyed expression, made it obvious that he was coming up much harder than I was. My mind was definitely bending and moving faster than normal, and the whole room had an acuity enhancement, but I was still lucid and comfortable in my head. This clarity did not stick around long, though, and about an hour and a half in, the come up anxiety started to get to me.

If I had been wiser, I would have put on some music and done something with my hands to ease myself into the trip. Instead, I sought a reason for my uneasiness, ignoring the fact that the acid come-up is like that. Something was off with the vibe, but I thought it was a personal, unresolved mental conflict, so I called my girlfriend for some support. I left Louis in the living room and laid down in my bedroom.

My love's voice had an immediate soothing effect, and as I shared some of my worries, she dissolved them and helped me towards peace. She reminded me that this was not unusual for the first part of a trip, and that I should try to ride it out and have fun. I told her I loved her and how thankful I was to have her, and she said she loved me back and that everything was good. I was relieved to have the relational side of my trip figured out, and felt ahead of the game. Usually, it would take me a couple hours to get steady with that, but now it was entirely secure early on. This gave me the freedom to trip without getting my feelings jumbled, and then I could always have that love to fall back on.

The call ended after a few minutes, and once I walked into the living room, the uneasy feeling returned. I reminded myself that it was just the come up, but something about Louis seemed off. His expression was a bit glum, but with him being much deeper in the acid realm than I was, I figured it would fade with time. I also considered that I could be projecting my own anxiety onto him, and I wondered what could make things better. I was quite antsy, and having spent a large part of the day in my small apartment, I longed to get outside for some fresh air.

The idea of going outside was a bit scary with the thought of being on LSD and getting lost in middle of the night, but I was confident enough in my mind to walk around. I suggested to Louis that we go for a walk, but he was hesitant. I saw two reasons for this: one was that his effects were coming on powerfully, and the other was that he did not trust me to navigate outside and keep us from getting lost. I tried to reassure him that I was lucid enough to stay safe and that a change of environment would be beneficial; sitting around was spiraling me towards an unpleasant mental state. Persuading him was difficult, but I did not see another option., and I was finally able to convince him.

Louis had to really collect himself before doing so, and I realized just how hard he was tripping when he started putting on his shoes. I had mine on in seconds, but he had to go through every action slowly and methodically. This made me feel brash; I was forcing my unconfident friend to go outside while on a heavy psychedelic experience. I knew it was for the greater good, though, as the environment was getting to both of us.

We carefully marched down the stairwell to the driveway and stared at the world. The wet asphalt glistened from the amber street light like sparkly water, overlain with damask patterns. Everything else was dark. The sky had a heavy cloud cover, and a light drizzle, which created a textured silence that contrasted all other sounds. The air was cold and damp, and the environment felt raw. It was starkly different from the mellow beige apartment we had spent the evening in, and was immediately refreshing. There was uncertainty between Louis and me about what we were actually doing out here, because standing in the driveway seemed weird. The fact that other people could be outside was also concerning; their perception of us could result in a police call or other form of intervention, so we had to look normal.

We decided that a walk around the block was simple enough, so we headed to the first corner of the sidewalk. I could not focus on the visuals or mental spaciness, as navigation demanded all my attention, but walking did feel very good. I was talking with Louis about how pleasant this was when I spotted two people on the sidewalk across the street. This grabbed my attention. I wondered if they saw us, and then I whispered to Louis that there were people. He got quiet and looked at them too. We couldn't just stop and stare; we had to keep walking, but it felt like we were doing something wrong and being watched. I proposed running up the hill into my backyard to Louis, and he contemplated it for a split second before recognizing the absurdity of the idea.

"Why would we do that? That would make us look super suspicious!"

I thought for a moment about this and then laughed at myself.

"What was I thinking? We're just out walking; all we have to do is go down the sidewalk."

Louis agreed, and I felt a sense of comedic relief at overcoming this weird moment of paranoia. We continued our stroll around the block, going by strange houses and black yards. Louis kept talking about how foggy it was, but I did not see any. To me, everything looked wet and clear with fine edges. I figured that Louis was deep in the acid haze, so I felt that I needed to demonstrate a level of proficiency for him to trust me not to freak out and get us lost. Neither of these things happened, but our walk ended very quickly. Once we were back in the driveway, I led us behind the garage where my garden was. This was a very private elevated area that overlooked a treeline. It was the perfect place to trip outside because nobody could see us and there was a view of the horizon.

We sat on the edge of a garden bed and looked out at the blotchy, black and gray sky. Silhouetted against it was a sumac tree, missing all of its leaves and reaching towards the clouds like a candelabra. The array of dancing branches seemed to sway and multiply and refused to be still. I asked Louis if he saw it too, and though he found the tree interesting, he seemed more focused on the psychological side of the trip. As he shared his ideas, the volume of my thoughts also expanded, and then we began discussing the nature of existence. I was particularly intrigued by the notion of filtered perception, specifically how my brain was creating my experience. The contrast between sobriety and an expanded perception created by LSD was very stark, and I felt that I deeply understood the potential for greater awareness. This substance seemed to reveal a broader picture of reality by increasing the capacity of my brain's thought capabilities. Because my mind was creating these realizations, they did not seem foreign. Instead, they seemed like previously unperceived layers of reality that had been revealed by the dissolving of a lens.

The implications of this concept remained to be seen, but I found great pleasure in contemplating what more there could be. I had not forgotten about my last LSD experience and the divine awareness that came with it, but now I had explored a fair bit of reality on this dosage, and so while the experience was new, I was not giving in to awe so quickly. The notion that my brain was actively processing information and creating my experience also gave me a kind of detached peace. I was still a part of the world, but because I was in a state of altered awareness, practicing the role of observer seemed wise. I did wonder what deeper links of reality Louis was perceiving, but at the same time, I felt confident in my dosage. Things were still pretty bizarre here, and before I could take a bigger dose to go further, I needed to get comfortable at this level.

The idea of a psychedelic substance revealing more layers of reality was not simply a theory in this trip, nor had it been in the previous one. This awareness was as convincing as everyday life because my sensory systems were still intact. I could hear the rain, feel the cold dew on my skin, navigate the environment, and smell the musk of the damp leaf piles, yet the fabric of reality was partially dissolved. It was a merging between psychedelia and life, with objects having characteristics in both realms. The sky, for example, had surging fractal patterns, but these did not strike me as alien. Instead, I felt that they had always been there, but I had just not perceived them before. It was still the sky that I had walked under all my life, but now it had the properties of a miasmic aura that I was existing in.

Louis and my conversation on existential subjects evolved quickly and moved at a pace that seemed impossible with sobriety. We were, however, on different wavelengths, so my understanding of topics was not as expansive as his. I would still be wrapping my head around concepts while he was already on to the implications of the conclusions of those thoughts. Our discussion remained enthralling, but most of the ideological intricacies were lost to the trip, as is their fate. I tried to hold onto what I could, but after an hour of sitting outside in the cold drizzle, both of us were ready to go in. I had a slight anxiety about returning to my apartment, but it seemed to be the only choice.

The off-feeling returned immediately, but once again, I could not figure it out. My mind was positively buzzing with the notions we had explored outside, but Louis seemed to have concluded his discussion on the subject. I figured that, because he was much deeper, he had some individual exploring to do that I could not completely comprehend. I still wanted to share and hold onto what I could from the prior contemplation on the nature of existence, so I called my girlfriend to tell her about it.

The notion of a biologically beneficial filtered perception of reality was not new to her; as a matter of fact, she had introduced me to the idea on one of my first acid trips. Now, having explored its implications extensively, I wanted to share the new ideas with her. I told her that I had frolicked in the magic novelty of the trip so far, and she was incredibly supportive, invested, and intrigued. This brought me untold levels of happiness. I felt so much love for her and the relationship we were building, along with a great love for my own life. My confidence in our love was steadfast, and I knew that the two of us cultivating this feeling of assurance and partnership could be identified as nothing else. She had emboldened me, and after some cozy talk, I ended the call with a feeling of supreme joy.

I returned to the living room, full of happiness, to see my friend with a gloomy expression. His eyes had dark circles under them, and a dreadful grimace dominated his face. I felt like a kid riding a rollercoaster who was watching his friend sitting on a bench who couldn't ride it. My trip was going so wonderfully, and I wanted the same for my friend, so I asked him: "What's wrong, man?"

"It's the end of time." Louis said, nodding with a serious look.

"What?" I replied, with a confused chuckle.

"It's the end of time. T....t...time is done," he said again with a grave tone.

"What are you talking about, dude?"

He thought for a moment and then began explaining, like a leader to a population facing extinction. "You are at the beginning of time, and I am at the bottom of time," He paused for a moment and continued "Or, you are at the beginning of the spiral of life, and I am at the end."

I still had no idea what he was talking about, or where he was getting this notion, but I was very well aware that we were both on acid. I knew that we had to figure this out, and I wanted to help him out of this bad place.

"I don't understand man. We are both alive; we are both in time. We're here hanging out in my apartment."

Silence followed for a moment as Louis seemed to contemplate this thought, before he said confidently, "I think I want to kill myself."

My mind raced. What's so bad that he thinks he wants to kill himself? Has he been dealing with these thoughts for a long time? Unlikely, we're on acid! He's having a bad trip! This is really serious though, like nothing I've ever had to deal with before. Every bad trip has always been me, never someone else. How do we handle this? This night has the potential to turn fatal.

"What!" I exclaimed in disbelief. "What are you

talking about man? We're on acid! We took LSD four hours ago. We're tripping."

"I know, but. . ." he said somberly. I had no experience dealing with someone considering suicide, nor did I want to get an of authority figure involved if we could make it out of this. This was the rule we followed with friends: exhaust all options before calling the police or an ambulance. Nobody wants to go to the hospital or be thrown in a cop car while they're tripping, and your friend's job is to help you ride out the bad experience. Louis had done the same for me on our last acid trip, helping me bike home safely and doing everything he could to quell my fears.

"Life is a gift! Life is great. Why would you want to kill yourself?" I asked, hoping to lead him out.

"If time is over, what's the point? We're just gonna disintegrate into dust anyway."

I shook my head. "No man, we took LSD at 7:18 pm and it's 11 pm now. It will end. We've just got a few more hours."

Louis visibly contemplated this fact, and hoping I could keep us moving in the right direction, I pulled up a music video to distract us: "Come a Little Closer" by Cage the Elephant. This may have been a mistake, but it was the first thing that came to mind, and I was enthralled by the emotional rollercoaster of the video. I understood the scenes from an entirely new point of view, seeing how the assumptions and choices we make are based on limited information, but when we get closer, we see things for what they truly are. I had watched this music video dozens of times in the past, but I was astounded at my unique understanding of it now. I knew that the creators were trying to get across the message of illusion, but exploring the depths of that message so quickly seemed only possible with psychedelics. I wondered what other music videos had hidden messages, and I wanted to share my new understanding with Louis, but he was only becoming more convinced that time was over. My next best idea was to just have him lie down and get away from his backpack, where I knew his knife was.

I suggested this and he agreed, so I watched him lie face down with his arms out in the middle of my bed. I felt empathy, and then dealt with a barrage of thoughts. The most important thing was keeping my friend from killing himself, and I had to stay vigilant for any more serious signs that he would attempt to do so. I was also getting freaked out by his talk of our different places on the spiral of life. Why did he think I was at the top? This desire to commit suicide was so incredibly foreign to me, especially now. Life was as sweet as candy, and I could only imagine how bad Louis thought his own life was to make him want to kill himself. I knew we had taken LSD, but I began searching for another reason why this was happening. Most disturbing was the fact that Louis lying in my bed. Truthfully, he was just trying to feel better, but to me it looked like he was trying to savor what I had.

I knew I was immensely blessed. I had a beautiful girlfriend, an amazing mom, good looks, and the world at my feet. I had not really thought about other people's perceptions of me, or whether anyone would compare their own life to mine, but I understood it on a whole new level at this moment. I was more fortunate than most and realized that Louis might envy what I have. I had been very open with him about my life and blessings, but had never once considered what that might look like compared to his life of hard work. I grew defensive and angry as I watched Louis lay in my bed and seem to savor my life, greatly considering what swapping lives would be like. These thoughts became overwhelming, and with my suicidal friend "safe" for the moment, I called my girlfriend once again and asked for her help.

She told me to make sure that there were no weapons around and that Louis was not near anything he could harm himself with. I told her I was hesitant to call anyone in authority because that might make things worse, and while she agreed, she said if things got dire, I should get my mom. I told her that I had been doing well and was trying to handle this situation the best I could. She was extremely familiar with my history of bad trips, and so hearing her perspective helped keep me calm and once again stoked the fire of appreciation I had burning for her.

While still on the phone, I heard Louis say something from my bedroom. It seemed quite distant, like most things sound on LSD. Your information processing is altered, so sounds and things that usually had clear origins and responses make very little sense. I heard him say something else and then I told my girlfriend that I loved her and that I would call again her if things got worse.

When I went back to the bedroom, Louis was sitting on the edge of the bed, saying he was okay. I did not believe him. I thought that he might be saying that he was okay so that my girlfriend would not suggest that I get additional intervention, so I pressed him a bit. I asked him why he wanted to kill himself, and he said he did not want to do so anymore. I knew he had not entirely figured out this bizarre headspace yet, but I hoped that talking more was the way to solve it. I also remembered that we had not eaten since 5 pm, so once he got up, I suggested that we drink some water and eat some food.

I wondered if hunger was the reason for his bad feelings. At the very least, eating would be a distraction, so I got a head of broccoli out of the fridge and went over to the sink with him to wash it off. For some reason, the drain plug was in and the sink was full of clear water. I had a foggy memory of putting water in the sink but could not remember why I had done so. It did, however, feel like a very "typical" thing to find on acid, so I rinsed off the broccoli before breaking off a stem and offering it to Louis.

He looked at it and shook his head, mumbling something about how I did not understand before tossing it into the sink with a splash. I was stunned and confused—

did he want something else to eat? Food seemed like the solution at this point, and eating had calmed my jitteriness. Louis, on the other hand, refused to eat and returned to the living room, so I followed. We sat down and our business was obvious: figuring out what the hell was wrong. I knew that his dosage had the potential to bring a range of effects, from depersonalization to ego death, and I figured that was what was happening.

Talking through these feelings was now the only way I saw to make things better, so we continued our discussion. Louis still believed that time had ended and that the essence of existence was over. We were two people who had somehow broken time and were now outside of it. This was the reason he wanted to kill himself—it was a means to end this sort of purgatory-like existence. I once again told him that time was still progressing and that we were very much in it. This did not convince him, though; he thought I had just not figured it out yet.

I did explore this notion of time being over, but it was so absurd that I simply could not entertain it. He was higher than me, and I could not get to that level. His experience gave me the idea of some kind of triangular space vortex composed of crimson red lines and psychedelic voids. I, however, was very much in the world, sitting by my fish tank and watching the guppies swim through the live jungle. This was the moment that I realized I was absolutely happy staying at this level. Louis was out in the hyperspace ocean, and though I was tremendously curious about what was out there, I was sure thankful I was in the shallows. Things were pretty peaceful here; perhaps not as exciting, but still divinely satisfying.

I thought that we were making progress on the subject of time ending, quickly moving away from talk of suicide, before Louis said that he had figured things out. I looked at him and he made a gun with his hand. "You're gonna do yourself," he said, pointing it at his head and then simulating a trigger pull, cocking his neck to the side.

"No! What are you talking about?" I yelled. "I'm not going to kill myself!"

His words deeply disturbed me. What if I was actually tripping and he said I should kill myself? Good thing I'm in my mind enough to know how God-awfully absurd he is talking. Even in some of my worst experiences, I had never considered suicide.

"Hmm," Louis said, very confused. I watched him continue to contemplate the way out of this broken time scenario, with my hope deteriorating by the second. Reason was not speaking to him, and I doubted that anything I said would really help. He would have to find his way out of this thought loop, and I had to make sure we stayed safe. I thought I might find a helpful video on the computer when Louis shot up off the couch and ran past me onto the porch. I had hardly even processed what had happened before I saw him looking out the window and shouting, "It's the end of time! Time is done!"

I hurried over to him and told him to quiet down.

"Do you see it?" he asked repeatedly, staring towards the sky.

"No, man, I don't see it. Let's go back in."

He stared out the window for another moment before reluctantly returning to the living room. I did not want him to shout out the window again because that would draw attention from the neighbors and that could cause huge problems. His actions had also been extremely sudden, and with the prior talk of killing and death, calming him down was vital.

The problem with talking to him was that his belief in time ending was unwavering. Everything I said to him just fit that idea, so where I would find a logical thought train out, he just used it as more fuel. The lack of progress frightened me, particularly with his casual attitude towards death. I pleaded the theory of ancestral contribution towards the current human form, but he just dismissed it and said it did not matter because time was over. Not only that, but both of us were going to die. I was really getting sick of it. The subject was slowly spiraling me into a dark place. I had to hold on to the threads of my sanity and see this thing out for both our sakes, but with his grim conclusions, I found my mind slipping.

"You kill me, I kill you." We had been in conversation when he said this, but I immediately lost the context. I had no understanding of why he was saying it, but it instantly shifted my mind. The air in the room became very clear. My chest burned, and my ears felt hot. My thoughts became extremely lucid, and all my senses sharpened.

During this time, I had expressed my outrage to Louis. This was my last grasp at hope of sanity. I said, "If you kill me, you go to jail." He nodded, like he understood, and said, "Yeah." The image of police taking him away in front of my house preceded the unthinkable punishment of life in prison. A crime so terrible that one would give up their entire life for it. It was inconceivable, yet here my friend sat, acknowledging the consequence of murder like a logical formula.

"Do you want to go to jail?" I asked in disbelief.

Louis looked at me with eyes of pain. In my heart, I did not believe he wanted to spend his life in jail, but my mind was too far gone. Logic was gone. The fact that we were on acid was gone. The only thing left was that he posed a mortal threat to me. What seemed to lie before us was a battle to the death. I did not want this, but with his threat to kill me, killing him was the only solution. I knew that this was not something I could do, and as my mind raced through possible courses of action, silent seconds of intensity ticked by.

Then Louis stood up, trying to act nonchalant. I knew that this was a method of assuming a more powerful position without putting me on guard. I immediately stood up and demanded that he sit back down. He refused, and then I bellowed from my stomach, "Sit back down!" He obliged this time, throwing his hands up to appear innocent. This was another ruse to get me to let my guard down and make me feel guilty for being so aggressive. I was not buying it.

I stared at him with intensity, at a loss for what to do next. I would not turn my back on him for even a second. I knew now that we were both helplessly deranged, but when I looked him in the eye, a switch flipped in my mind. I realized that was in true, mortal peril, so I bolted into the stairwell. He laughed and screamed behind me, making me feel like I was running out of a basement from a monster. My feet pounded down each step like a survival minigame until I ripped the door open and launched myself into the driveway. What was I going to do? Louis would surely hunt me down if he could find me the neighborhood. The garden was the best spot—I could see all the ways in and launch an ambush if he were to come back.

I shimmied my way between the two garages along a concrete-block path before emerging in the wet and dark garden. I searched for a weapon and grabbed a rusty metal fence pole before crouching down and making myself completely silent. I heard every single raindrop; every surface they touched and the different tones they made. This was it—the fight for my life. Combat philosophies and survival strategies surged through my mind. I vividly recalled my brief martial arts instruction, along with Bruce Lee and Jackie Chan movies. Everything I had learned from them would pay off now. This was my destiny; I had been trained through countless hours of player-versus-player video games. From gun battles in Call of Duty and strategic positioning and opponent reading in League of Legends, to chaotic Grand Theft Auto fights and Minecraft survival—it was all for this purpose.

I scanned the environment, taking note of the access points leading to my position and what I would do to cover them. My fear of Louis grew as I relived those moments in the apartment, and I could not shake the idea of him stabbing me in the throat, bloodying the pure white Hollister sweatshirt I was wearing. I believed that would be extremely gratifying for him because the sweatshirt was a symbol of what I was living for. I would often wear it to high school, as well as loan it to my girlfriend, and staining it with my blood would be a grotesquely poetic end to those things. He knew this and wanted it.

The image of my slashed throat gushing blood played over and over in my head, fueling my desire to survive and my vilified perception of Louis. My belief in his desire to kill me grew by the second as I pieced together our past and now saw clear signs of his intentions. The purpose of our player versus player games was for him to learn my strategies, and his goal had always been to have me let my guard down. This was the real reason I had distrusted him on our last trip—he wanted to get us lost so that I would be vulnerable.

I was most disturbed by the solution: killing him. I knew that his murderous intent was not trip-exclusive, but that the trip had accelerated destiny. That meant that he would be a threat to me for the rest of our lives, and so the only way for me to survive would be his end. I did not have the same bloodthirsty intent, however—just a blazing desire to live. This meant that I would be in the role of prey, unable to set the time or place. I would have to be on guard, ready to defend my life from Louis at any moment. This required perfect awareness and observation, so I took note of every facet of the environment. I knew that Louis was sneaky and cunning, so I took an inventory of everything around me, highly suspicious of any change.

Never before had I been in a position like this, and though my last acid trip had brought forth fierce survival instincts in me, this one was unveiling a whole new realm of ancestral awareness embedded deep in my genome. I was confident in myself and felt the fire of endurance burn in my heart as I considered the love and life I was fighting for. I would do anything to win, but Louis knew how much I cherished life, and that would make my death at his hands that much more satisfying for him. He was the epitome of raw and sinister evil, and I could not be near him. But, he was now in my apartment, with all my belongings, tools, memorabilia, and things I cared for. My cat, my fish, all my sensitive personal documents—available to him. This could not stand.

I knew I would be a fool to walk back up to an ambush. I was already on the brink of insanity, or in the eye of it, so any more time Louis and I spent together posed a threat to both of us. I considered my options and remembered that I had a phone. I pulled it out and tried to conceal the light; I did not want to give away my position. Fortunately, it was fully charged. I thanked myself for the foresight, but was unsure what to do next. Calling 9-1-1 would be a mistake—that was only an option if he actively began trying to kill me. Besides, I would probably look like the insane one, standing out in the rain with a rusty pole, rambling on about my murderous friend. Making any call would produce sound that could give my position away, and with Louis potentially lurking around any corner, I feared the repercussions. After long consideration, with disturbing thoughts of Louis snooping through my documents, I decided to call my mom.

  I hastily explained the situation to her, and when she pressed me on where I was, I told her that I was somewhere safe not far from home. Then she offered to go up into my apartment and talk to him, and I advised great caution. She was sober and could handle the situation better, but I loved her dearly. I feared for her safety, but I told her I really wanted him gone. I asked her to call me if anything bad happened, and then, after she assured me that it was okay, we hung up. A few seconds later, I heard the clanging of an aluminum screen door open and immediately crouched into a defensive position. Then I realized that it was my mom going up to my apartment. I said a prayer, and then listened for my screen door to close before the sound of drizzling rain was all I could hear.

Still moments passed as I wondered if I had just sentenced my mother to her fate. Then, I realized that Louis would use manipulative strategies to coerce my mother into thinking that I was the delusional one, which would ultimately result in her taking his side. But this was my mother—she would not disregard my fear so carelessly. Nevertheless, I understood now that I had introduced a new dynamic to Louis and my death match. I was appalled by the idea that he might involve her and play on my emotional attachment to her. I could not let him win her over, as this would surely seal my fate.

I heard the clanging metal door creak open and then crouched low to hide myself. I waited until I heard my mother's car doors open and close before peeking my head through the narrow corridor between the garages. The headlights of the car burned into the night, and my heart soared as I watched them disappear down the driveway. He was gone-thank God for my amazing mother. I waited for another few seconds to catch my breath before tiptoeing down the path.

I returned to the duplex porch and shouted, "Hello!" as I opened my screen door. No response. I slinked up the stairwell, and then craned my neck through the upper doorway into my apartment. I didn't see Louis at first, but then a sick feeling came over me when I saw his things still scattered around the room. I turned back down the stairs and ran to the garden. There was no way that he was gone for good without his brown backpack and vaporizer. I knew he would be back for them.

I scurried along the path to the cold and damp garden before crouching down with a view of the driveway. Sure enough, my mom's car pulled back in, and I knew that not enough time had passed for her to bring Louis to his dorm. I watched with dread as the two of them got out of the car before quickly concealing myself. I heard the metal door open once again, followed by still seconds of silence. Then my hip started buzzing and I pulled out my phone to see that it was my mom calling.

"Why is he still here?" I asked frantically.

"He had to get his stuff. I told him to stay upstairs."

"I saw that. Please, I just want him gone."

"I know, I know, but I don't think it's a good idea to bring him back there now."

A moment of compassion followed this statement as I wondered what kind of terror Louis would face wandering around a private Christian college on 420µg of LSD at 12 am. It did not matter, though—living was more important.

I pleaded with my mom, but then she invited me inside. It was cold and dark out here; I was shivering and in bare feet, but it was preferable to death. I told her that I was staying outside, but she pressed and told me I would feel better if I came in. I did not want to, as I felt safe where I was, but I wondered what I would do in the long term. Was I going to stay out here, on guard, all night? That would be a mistake. There was strength in numbers, and rest would keep my mind sharp.

I decided that I would go inside after my mom assured me that Louis was not there. I could not just walk in the front door, though—that would make me ripe for an ambush. I would go around the back. I told my mom this before hanging up. Then I heard the soft rain again, and Bruce Lee came to mind. I considered his superior fighting ability as a means for survival. My encounter with his movies had not been by chance, nor the martial arts obsession that followed soon after. All those techniques were at play now. I had paid close attention and practiced, and now I saw them through a completely different lens. No longer were they simply exercises and interesting techniques: they were the means of survival. Their application was to give me life by giving me the ability to dominate combat.

I was in a fighting state, highly aware and ready to counter anything. The sound of a wood block being hit by a mallet played over and over in my mind, like some kind of battle metronome. My teeth replicated the sound, clinking together with the purpose of analyzing my entire external environment. It was time to make a break for the house, but opening the gate would be noisy and revealing, so I vaulted over the top of the chainlink fence, making a clanging sound.

I moved quickly. This was the only indication I had given of my location. I bolted to the door and knocked on it incessantly. Then, through the French door windows, I saw a man with poofy hair and a scowling, fat pink face. It was my stepdad. He was burly and intimidating, but I felt safe. He opened the door and I stepped inside.

"Louis is trying to kill me," I said with panicked honesty.

He paused for a moment.

"Is he on drugs?"

"Yeah."

"Call the cops on him."

The callous attitude of my stepdad soothed me. He was an ally who was undoubtedly on my side. Straight forward to the solution and a force to be reckoned with. When I admitted to him that we had both taken drugs, his idea of calling the cops changed, but his strength did not. I felt safe here in his household. Then my mom came in, and he returned to the living room, where he was watching a war movie.

I started explaining the situation to my mom, telling her what Louis had said and how the trip had gone bad. I told her that I did not feel safe around him, nor did I trust myself, and that he needed to go home. She was understanding but seemed unwilling to bring him back to his college. Then I heard the side door open, and Louis filled the entryway. I immediately distanced myself, and my mom stood between us. She began trying to mediate, but I was having absolutely none of it. Louis had a crazed smile that filled my heart with dread, and as I listened to the distant voice of my mother trying to de-escalate the situation, I understood why he was smiling. He had somehow convinced my mom that we should still be together—that I had misunderstood him and that more time to talk would fix the situation. He had tricked her, just like I predicted.

"No! No! No! I want him gone! Get rid of him!" I shouted. "He wants to kill me!" My voice was gravelly with desperation, and my neck felt swollen and pink.

Louis had formed a relationship with my mother to further his sinister plot, and now only my stepdad was on my side. I could not let this stand, so I continued insisting with ferocity that Louis needed to go, until finally my mom sent him back upstairs. She would not be bringing him home tonight, so I went and locked every door before retreating to my mom's room. Then I sat on guard on the edge of her bed for two hours, watching and waiting.

As I thought about what I could do to avoid being killed, hundreds of scenarios played through my mind, all different ways that Louis would kill me. They varied in grotesqueness and intensity, like a buffet of death, each satisfying Louis in a unique way. I asked myself why he wanted to kill me, and adopted a self-centered perspective. My life was sweet and immensely blessed, and I thought that, from his perspective, I was undeserving of it. I knew that we were both on LSD, but there was too much convincing evidence to write it off as just tripping. I knew that morning sobriety would bring clarity, but I did not believe that was where this game would end.

    I observed my past with Louis. Our conversations, activities, sketchy encounters, and unspoken communications. These all fit the narrative that pointed to a sinister end, and I saw tonight's trip as an acceleration of fate because of what Louis had said: the spiral of life had ended. We had been on it for our entire relationship, and now its conclusion was one of our deaths. This was inescapable, and if it did not happen tonight, it would tomorrow. I saw the image of Louis driving a knife into my throat in his college parking lot and wondered about what death would be like in that place. I thought about the appalling news story, his capture and incarceration. Never before had I thought of someone as possessing such evil, nor myself as one with a high bounty.

    I slowly came to terms with the potential for my murder, and I determined that I would handle the situation if it were to come before me, but that I could not remain at a tension all night. I also knew that exhaustion would make me more vulnerable, so I laid back and breathed. I shut my eyes and saw blackness before a horizontal crimson line formed. This was a timeline, and I followed it to a point where there was an X and a skull, signifying the end of a life. I considered the implications of this; all of the people who had met their end at the hands of another, and the complete cessation of their lineage. The image of a desolate, archaic Japanese village then filled my view. Two swordsmen crossed paths, and one emerged victorious. This was a brutally raw demonstration of the reality of combat.

Fighting had been a focus of mine for the past year, from video games and martial arts research to the variety of melee weapons I had amassed and trained with. I had not perceived Louis's role until now, but the two of us had faced multiple dangerous situations. These included nearly being hit by a cop car, terrors from the previous Halloween of gangs and clowns, our visceral acid bike ride, and intense outdoor sports. It was more than that, though—every single thing about our relationship fit the treacherous pattern. I realized this from a piece of psychedelic geometry forming before me that looked like a massive gear with many polygonal teeth. Its inside glowed with metallic pink and green damask patterns to orange and teal sacred geometry, like the shimmer from a gemstone mass being hit by light through water.

This was a pattern of existence. A hyperdimensional, geometric depiction of physical events, showing the connections between them. It was a representation of the "bigger picture." This information was not linguistic, but was instead like a hyperspace tesseract whose components were manifestations of entire three-dimensional events. It was not standing alone, but was rather like a piece of a much larger psychedelic puzzle. I felt like I was holding it very close to my face, unable to see the whole object. Perhaps I had the power to take a step back, but with how vital the information from this piece of the pattern was, I thought it foolish to expand. Besides, what kind of sinister puzzle has a section in it where I face murder? Do I really want to see the full scope of that?

Maybe stepping back and seeing how this pattern of existence fit into the bigger picture could bring me solace, but I did not want to accept that reality. I was a living, breathing creature, not some prey destined for slaughter. My life was in my own hands, not in those of some secret cosmic recipe. And even if it was, I did not care. I would fight my way to the bitter end and do everything in my power to win. I recognized this as an ancestral feeling. It was deeper and more raw than any emotion I had experienced—a fire of ferocity that had burned in all my ancestors up to me to ensure survival.

The patterns of existence—this phrase repeated itself over and over in my head as I remembered all of Louis's and my relationship through the lens of his malicious intent. It was clear to me. I didn't have a fear of acid; rather I was thankful for it, because it had accelerated my destiny and shown me the truth. The problem was, of course, that the trip was not over, and was not going to end in the morning. It was up to me to give myself the best chance at survival with this new perspective.

I laid there next to my mom for two hours, slowly coming to terms with the reality of trying to survive my friend wanting to kill me. My body was now weary, and my mind numb. I knew that I needed to rest, but in order to do so, I had to accept the possibility of my murder. I could not spend all night afraid. I was in a safe location, so the only thing left was to make a plan for what I would do if Louis were to come downstairs. It was up to me now. I had to take control of my survival. My love for life was worth it, as was my love for my family and friends. I would fight ferociously and equip myself with the tools to prosper.

My mom eventually suggested that I go to the extra bedroom to sleep, which was upstairs next to my apartment. It would put me uncomfortably close to Louis, although the room did not have any access to my apartment. I was still so sure that he was up there, so I procrastinated and called my love, telling her about all that had happened. She was the only one who seemed to believe that Louis was trying to kill me, and she affirmed my choices. I was immensely thankful that I had a partner I could count on and trust to support me when things went bad. She had already helped me through countless trying experiences, and though this one was still traumatic, I was not panicking about my loss of sanity. Our relationship was secure, as was my faith in myself, so I was able to enjoy a brief talk with her about love. She was a reminder of the beauty I was fighting for.

By around 2 am, she was tired and telling me that it was time to go to sleep. I thought this might be the last time I would talk to her, so I told her how dearly I loved her and how important she was to me. I knew I had to let her sleep, so I reluctantly said goodbye and chose to face the next part of the trip: going into the spare bedroom. The stairway leading up to it was by the dining room, and that was the only way in. The room was small, no bigger than 80 square feet, tucked away on the second floor. It sat right next to my apartment and was close enough that you could hear someone talking on the other side, but separated by a few inches of drywall. The only way anybody could get to you was by going through the downstairs first.

That was exactly what I thought Louis had done, and that he was hiding in the stairwell for an ambush. I stared at the closed door leading up to the room; it did not appear unusual or tampered with, but I knew that if I was going to attack someone, I would make things look as normal as possible. I quietly grabbed the handle and jerked the door all the way open and hid behind it. I waited for a moment, and then peered around it—the stairs were empty. Then, I slinked up them with my back pressed against the wall until I was on the second level. Another door separated me from the spare room, so I paused for a moment before forcing it open and inserting myself into the room. No one was there.

I looked around the room, charting every corner and hidden space. I checked the closet, under the bed, behind the door, next to the cabinet, and then back down the stairwell. He was not up here, and I was as far away from him as

I could be in the house in terms of accessibility. He would have to go all the way down my apartment stairs, break into my parent's house, and then go up the spare bedroom stairs. And even then, I would have the upper hand for an ambush. I had to accept that I was in the best location I could be, given the circumstances, so I laid down in bed and shut my eyes. Everything was quiet at first, and then a kaleidoscopic tunnel emerged from the blackness and began pulling me in. Tesseract shapes blended with green beams of light surged about in my visual field, and that same familiar pattern of existence pulsed in and out of my consciousness. This was a treasure that had been revealed to me to protect my life, and although I knew my mind was warped, I was grateful for it.

I wondered what the bigger picture looked like, how this particular pattern fit into my entire life's puzzle. I knew I could not see it now, though; my dose was too low. I did not think I was ready, either. I had to process my current realization and take appropriate measures before even considering what would come next. The reality now was that Louis wanted to kill me, and if that did not happen tonight, it would happen tomorrow when I took him home. If not then, another time. His talk of the cycle of life beginning and ending had only one resolution: a life beginning, and the other ending.

Killing Louis was not the solution to this; that would just end two lives. My only course of action was to prepare myself. To be vigilant, protected, and cautious so that when he did try, he would not succeed. This was an entirely new approach to things. I could no longer be naive and careless. I could no longer take my safety for granted; life was far too important to me. I had so many aspirations and so much love to give, and in order to do so, I had to take appropriate measures. This was the way forward, regardless of what would happen tomorrow.

Now, my head hurt, not because I was dehydrated, but because I had thought so much. It felt like my brain had been on overdrive, thinking about nine things at once for the last 12 hours. I had contemplated more in ten minutes than I usually did in an entire day, and now all my mind wanted was to rest. There still seemed to be an infinity of thought to explore, but doing so required a fresh mind. I was exhausted and had accepted that I was safe. It was time to sleep.

***

I woke up around noon without any memory of dreaming, and my mom was there, giving me a protein bar and some water. I had only been awake for a few minutes before she suggested that I go talk to my friend. I was calm now, and though still shaken, not nearly as afraid. I gathered my confidence and left my parents, heading up to face Louis. It was a peculiar feeling, opening my apartment door to see a friend who had scared me out of it. This was my home, yet here I was coming in feeling like a stranger. I did not hear anything while I walked up the stairs, and then there he was, sitting on the couch with a vibe of tired modesty. I did not feel threatened or nervous, but I did have a desire to talk.

Only a few minutes had passed before I realized the depth of his experience. He described it as one of the most intense acid trips he had been on, and based on his description, it sounded like he had gone through true ego death. I felt immediate empathy but still remained firm in my decision; separating us was the best choice. I was also very grateful that I had only taken two tabs, and that he had not hurt himself. I did feel like I had abandoned my friend during a trying part of his trip, but he did not hold that against me. He did express concern with my portion of the experience, seeming confused about how I got the idea that he wanted to kill me. Our stories differed a bit; he saw my freak-out as unwarranted, while I remained adamant in my choices reasoning. This did not seem to matter, though—the trip was over and it would take both of us time to process it. We would certainly be talking about it later, but for now, there was no ill will.

We talked for about an hour, and I could not get over the irony of how long we had planned this trip and how badly it had gone. Years had passed since the very first time Louis and I daydreamed about tripping together, yet when the time finally came around, it was traumatizing. I wondered if things would have gone better if we had tripped on a different day, or if my new perception of Louis was somehow inevitable. I did not like the idea that he was evil, and I knew that my fear of him was attributed to things he had said while tripping, but I was still suspicious. I was unsure if he was not remembering the night correctly, suppressing it, or simply denying it, but I could not forget that moment in the downstairs kitchen. I was so sure of his malicious intent, but when I tried to tell my mom, he denied it and acted innocent. What else could he do? Admit to wanting to kill me? Denial was his only option, but of course, I did not believe him at that moment.

    I tried to push out these thoughts and focus on the facts: we had been tripping on a lot of acid, neither of us had made physical attempts on each other's lives, and now we were sitting together the morning after as friends. The night had gone seriously wrong, but neither of us was suffering from permanent psychosis or longstanding after-effects. All things considered, we were fortunate to come out mostly unscathed. Had I run around the neighborhood panicking, or rode away in the car, or gotten the police involved, we would be in a very different position. Louis had not harmed himself, and now we were talking about the trip, trying to figure out what the hell went wrong.

    We could only explore so much together before the need for individual contemplation became clear, so we eventually decided that it was time for Louis to go home. He packed up his things and then took one look back at the soft beige apartment he had spent the bizarre night in before heading down the stairs. I followed close behind, and then we walked out onto the driveway that had been grotesquely distorted the night before. The world looked "normal" now, but no less weird than last night. There were the houses that we had walked by, along with the uneven sidewalk and soggy lawns. They all had the same characteristics as they had the night before: oddly ominous and seemingly fleshy, like architecture of the void. We had both been here, inside of this space. The world was not different now; we were the difference. It was all, disturbingly, the same.

    I asked Louis, less poetically, if he understood this, and to my surprise, he did exactly. He remembered the entire block being blanketed in a haze with beings in it that looked like the no-face Kaonashi of the Spirited Away anime—a white, oval-shaped mask with triangles above and below its black circles for eyes. This description made me even more chillingly perplexed with his trip, and then I remembered a sort of maroon triangular prism existing in a sparkly black space that represented him. Louis had been to the void where time ceased to exist, perceiving the spirals of life and death and experiencing an entirely different world. The more I heard and thought about this, the more thankful I was that I had stayed at my dosage, and I seriously questioned whether I would ever go that deep.

    The drive back to Louis's college was relatively quiet, and it did not feel all that different than any other. We vaped, enjoyed some rap music, and then were in the campus parking lot. I remembered what I had thought the night before—this is where he stabs me in the throat. It did not happen. He got out of the car, grabbed his bag from the back seat, and then came back over to the passenger side door to say goodbye. I smiled and wished him the best, feeling sympathy for his rough trip, and then asked if we would hang out soon. He said yes, and I felt my heart warm; we were still friends, with plans to spend time together, despite a treacherous night. We said goodbye, and then I drove off, curious and overwhelmed about what the future would hold.

Chapter 9

The Last Trip

Following the acid trip with Louis, I took a break from psychedelics for over three months. This hiatus came not only from fear, but also because my schedule had filled up. I was now taking a few credit hours at a local college, and when I was not studying, I was playing a lot of League of Legends or visiting my girlfriend in another state. This, combined with heavy nicotine vaping and abusing weed and caffeine, put me in a particularly odd frame of mind. I did not really know where I was going. The biology classes at college were meant to continue expanding my interest in horticulture, and I was pretty good at League, making it into the top 3% of players, but something was missing. I did not have a clear path because I had not set many goals. Most of what I was doing was rooted in feeling good, searching for adventure, satisfying the expectations of society, and love. I loved my girlfriend and I loved plants. League felt good, and college was sort of expected of me, but I was not happy.

My discontentment came to a peak in late March of 2018. I had passed my classes and left college, but with winter keeping me inside, I was trying to figure out what I wanted to do with my life. College was not it. Even going part-time had significantly upped my vaping and energy drink habits, and instead of school inspiring me, it just gave me an excuse to get high in my free time. That said, I had not started college with "good intent." At 6 am, the morning before my very first day of class, I smoked a bowl of the hybrid strain, Agent Orange, and figured that was just how I was going to make it through. I had been completely over school since I had graduated from high school in 2016, but I figured I could dope my way through and learn some things about growing plants while getting credits. Besides, the classes were not that expensive, and it gave me something to say when people asked what I was doing.

However, the courses I had to take to get a degree were tedious, and I honestly feared what another semester would do to my body. The nicotine binging was the worst; I even had a classmate remark on the clouds of vapor that would plume into the parking lot every time I got out of my car. I eventually revealed to him the full extent of my activities: that I was also bringing a propane torch to school and dabbing in my car, along with the occasional microdose of acid. I was high most of the time, and school still sucked, so I figured that it was time to do something else. Maybe I would go pro at gaming and build on my Youtube channel, or use my plant knowledge to construct some kind of greenhouse and start growing weed. Both were compelling ideas, and I did spend a lot of my time figuring out how to act on them. The problem was that the rut of intoxication and nothingness was far more attractive and ate up a huge amount of my time.

Apathy and a rejection of culture fueled my romance with dissociation, but I was not a drinker or a partier. I avoided large social situations and preferred heavy cannabis use alone or with a small group of close friends. I had no interest in meeting new people, playing party games, watching movies, or going to music venues. I desired to be high and withdrawn into the void, seeking peace and treasures from a different realm. I hated the culture of sex and violence that surrounded me, along with its love of money and materialistic passions, so I hid from it and used my hatred of it to justify my actions. I did not find happiness, though. Instead, I found comfort in a kind of familiar suffering, using moral philosophy to convince myself that degeneracy was a natural response to the world I lived in.

That worldview manifested itself in me as chronic cannabis and nicotine use, countless hours of video games, and a lack of care about anything other than my girlfriend and family. All this, along with the dozen psychedelic experiences and pounds of weed I had smoked in the past two years contributed to my perceptions. My apathy and detachment were certainly more extreme now, but they had always been a part of me. I sensed that my actions were not producing a healthy state of mind and that I was slipping deeper into addiction, but the way out was not clear.

Then one evening, my vape stopped working. I had the option of going to buy a cheap one from a gas station, but I ended up just smoking a bunch of weed and figuring I would deal with it later. I felt a bit weird, but not especially upset. This was the first time in three years that I did not have a working nicotine device at my disposal, and I wondered what the following morning would be like. More than a few of my friends were self-admittedly addicted to vaping, and with all the rumors about nicotine withdrawals, I thought that I would suffer the next day. Maybe then I would hop online and buy a new one, or see if I could just tough it out, but quitting cold turkey seemed foolish. That said, weed was pretty damn good by itself, so I figured that I could just smoke more often and possibly have more of its pure effects shine through.

  The following morning came, and I woke up without a headache or serious craving, but taking a big puff of tasty tropical e-liquid did sound delicious. I wanted to see what the day would be like without it, though, so I just made some tea and enjoyed the morning a bit more sober than usual. This was pleasant, but I was confronted with the same questions I had been dealing with for the past few months: what was I doing with my life? How was I going to make money, and when was I going to stop spending all my time stagnating? I did not know. Instead of my sobriety answering these questions, however, it made them more pressing.

  That was when I decided to find the mushrooms I had gotten from a college classmate the previous semester. We had become friends early on, and after some exam prep together, I revealed my psychedelic experience Youtube channel to him. He took an interest in the topic, and after a few conversations about it, he offered me the mushrooms. They had been sitting in my freezer for a few months, alongside the leftover void realm acid from the scary trip with Louis. I really had no plans to take anything powerful after that trip, especially given my current mental state, but I could not turn down something as rare and special as mushrooms.

I had been thinking about them, though, and wanted a trip to show me something new, but the time never seemed right. I was a firm believer in preparing for psychedelic trips and being entirely confident in my mental state prior to them, but this was a unique occasion. I had been in a funk for a while, and with my vape dying, maybe I could get a new perspective on things. My intention was to find something tangible to focus on: a goal, a new project, a spiritual quest, or some kind of innovative idea to pursue. I also knew that mushrooms had the potential to kick addictions. I did not have a great plan for taking them, however. I spent most of that day wondering if I should trip before finally deciding around 4 pm that the woods would be a good setting, and figured at the very least I could enjoy some natural solitude.

The choice to trip was a bit of a Hail-Mary. I knew very well that it could go terribly wrong, especially because my mind was unsteady, but I wanted to feel better. I was sick of being where I was, so I chewed up the mushrooms and prepared myself for the experience. They were only 1.5 grams, though my college buddy had said they were an especially strong strain. I was not going to smoke weed, and I assured myself that I was well enough to handle the experience and that the mushrooms were kind. I grabbed my phone and slipped on my shoes before heading outside to begin the mile walk to the park.

The world was not especially interesting. It was just lots of houses, cars, asphalt, burnt lawns, and boring businesses. I was not really focused on it, though; all I could think about was what the trip was going to be like. I had not taken mushrooms since that 5 gram all-nighter in high school with Slater, and with multiple freaky acid trips under my belt, I was happy to go back to something organic. That said, the line between sobriety and tripping was becoming very gray. I could not tell if the way that my mind was working was because of the mushrooms, or if I was just thinking that I was having perceptual distortions.

By the time I made it to the park, I was beginning to come up. The summer day was mild and blue skied, and I chose the ridge trail surrounded by tall oak trees. I was still up in my head, distracted by unhappiness and asking myself, 'Where had I gone wrong?' My whole intention in embarking on this trip was to feel better, and now here I was, still searching for answers. I believed that mushrooms would reveal some kind of path to me that would bring work, money, and success.

They were not having it though. Instead, I sat down and thought about how I had been spending my time. 6-8 hours in front a computer screen playing video games and vaping on nicotine nearly every day for over a year. I had no doubt that these activities were unhealthy, but I was doing them because I did not know what I wanted to do with my life. Then it occurred to me—I needed to give.

"I need to give," I said to myself, over and over, until I was brought to tears. My fixation was on self, and I realized that with all the time I had spent pleasing myself, instead I could have helped so many people. I had the power to change lives, yet all I had been pursuing was trying to make myself feel good. The realizations came in waves, as I was both ashamed and humbled at what I was being shown. The contrast to my initial intent reinforced this lesson even further, as my only focus on the way here had been on myself.

I cried my whole heart out, and the tears felt good. I was not in pain, rather I was being released. This was the first time in as long as I could remember that I had allowed myself this kind of emotion, and it felt like years of suppression were finally breaking free. Words of self-criticism and negativity that I had tormented myself with for years spiraled in my mind and were washed away. My emotions surged with staggering power and were beautifully raw. There was no inhibition, doubt, or shyness—it was all pure feeling.

The purging tears continued for a half hour as I sat there on a tree stump in the middle of the woods. I was immersed in the experience of catharsis, but I feared what would happen afterwards. I could not stay here crying all day. I knew that the whole point of this experience was to help me live a happier life, but the unknown of what came next scared me. So, I decided to call my mom and tell her about what I was struggling with. Beyond the trip, my problem of figuring out what to do with my life was not an unusual one, and my mom affirmed that I did not need to rush it. I could take it day by day, and should most importantly appreciate the present moment.

So that's what I did: I gathered myself and accepted everything that had just happened. I did not rush to any conclusions, decide on any extreme revelations about life, or discover some kind of new mantra that would help me conquer the world. All I decided was that I needed to give more, and I needed especially to focus on enjoying the present moment, which was beautiful. The forest floor was a colorful mosaic of orange, yellow, and brown, and there was a soft summer breeze that revitalized my skin. The air felt like love in my lungs, and all around me were tall trees producing that air. Their canopy branches were covered in emerald leaves and contrasted geometrically with the cerulean sky.

I followed the ridge trail, immersed in the majesty around me. Squirrels playfully darted around trees, and the soothing songs of birds melodized with the sound of branches blown by the wind. I needed to head home though; my psyche was vulnerable and I wanted to relax.

Leaving this serene setting felt wrong. I loved it out here, and felt more connected to nature than in my small apartment. At home, there were plenty of strange objects and man-made creations, whereas here in the forest, everything seemed to be in its rightful place. There was serenity in the casual chaos of nature, and I felt no great need to do anything here.

I reminded myself that this place had been here for a long time and that I could come back to enjoy it in the future. Leaving was still disheartening, but I knew I had to go, so I gave the forest a vigorous, loving farewell before returning to the sidewalk. I was still in an appreciative mindset, and now the way home seemed completely different. I was hardly thinking intentionally at all, and instead was trying to take in the fast-moving environment. Even the little patches of grass between the sidewalk and road were interesting, and I could not believe how many new things I was seeing. Lawn ornaments, landscaping, cars, people, architecture, the sky and clouds, treetops and birds; it was happening all around me. I was not trying to make sense of it all, but instead served as a kind of simple witness to so much that was out of my control.

I considered what my role was in all of this happening, and found great satisfaction at its innocence. I was just a walker, heading down the sidewalk, without any need to do anything but avoid cars. Nobody would think twice if I stayed on the concrete squares that went in a straight line, and as long as I kept moving, I had the lovely privilege of just observing the world. The contrast of my current perception was so stark when compared to the walk to the park that I truly realized my mind's ability to detach me from the moment. None of what I was seeing now had been taken into account before, and the most thrilling part of this realization was its implications for my happiness. I had the power to turn my thoughts towards negativity and complain about this emission-filled, sun-scorched, asphalt plane, yet I was happy because I had made the choice to be. The world was truly magnificent and filled with so much that I had the gift of experiencing.

When I got close to home, I started to get anxious. I believed that this was because of my habit of returning to my old ways. My apartment would be the same as when I had left it, but what would I do when I got up there? I did not want to play video games, and I was not especially interested in philosophizing or getting creative. I felt tired and emotionally spent. When I entered my apartment, it felt stagnant and dry. The rays of the afternoon summer sun bleached my walls and carpet and brought me a familiar feeling of dread. What was I doing? Another day was coming to a close, and here I was in my apartment, just watching it go by. The combined feelings of boredom, anxiety, deterioration, and lack of direction compounded and welled in my heart.

I caught myself before going too far, and I reminded myself of what I had just gone through—a cathartic experience in the woods. Now was not the time to try to figure out all the answers to life, and with my mind vulnerable from mushrooms, treading lightly and acting with compassion towards myself was the path to take. So, I just walked around my apartment and looked at all my things: tiny wooden boats, jewelry and baubles on my dresser, trophies, plants in chalky terracotta pots, and shiny rocks. Everything seemed very ordinary and unthreatening, and I loved this. There were no objects that gave me fear or dread, and the only pressing matter was the basket of folded laundry my mom had left on my bed.

    I started putting my clothes away, and began spiraling down a self-critical thought-stream, berating myself for not doing my chores. I stopped this thought process by choosing to appreciate each piece of clothing. Then I spotted my black and white cat, Darma. She sat properly on the edge of the bed, half asleep and content. I went over to her and gently laid my palm on her silky coat. She let out an approving mew, and I slowly and gently petted her before picking her up and lying down on my bed with her on my chest. I continued petting her and felt my heart warm as her purrs radiated through my body. She was a small, fragile life form that I cared for and loved, who was waiting for me here at home.

    I lay there with the cat falling asleep on my chest and observed my room. It was a small box with rectangular glass panes that revealed the sunny treetops and blue sky. I liked the purpose of windows: to let in light and show the outside. They struck me as purely aesthetic additions to a house, and got me wondering about all the things people own for that sole delight factor. I had many things in my room that were beautiful because they were not utilitarian. What good or practical need did the crystal and tiny wooden boat sitting on my cabinet serve? None—they were just simple additions that I bought because they looked cool. The whole point of their creation was to be pretty, which made them beautifully useless.

As much as I loved nature, there was something settling about being in this calm and familiar environment. I came to appreciate my apartment for what it was: a quiet, safe place with things I loved in it. As a creation of humans, I considered how tailored this space was for me. All of the details, like doorway size, ceiling height, windows, closets, and paint were all for me, a human being. This fact touched my heart because this place was created not just to protect me and keep me warm, but also to be inviting, pleasing, and comfortable. And, I had contributed to these elements by carefully placing furniture and artwork, all for the purpose of creating a nice, inviting space.

I recognized that I was still tripping, but I did not feel especially out of my mind. My thoughts did not feel alien or strange compared to sobriety. I felt entirely capable of having these same thoughts when I was not tripping, but their depth and speed were unmistakably increased now. My perception was, however, more clear. The world seemed much more innocent now, and discovering my role in it was easy. I was a life that needed compassion, love, and care just like everyone else. I experienced the world through my senses and was able to control so little of it. I was small, but significant, and composed of pure energy and emotion that were expressed through physicality. My spirit was eternal, and I had come from infinity, but now I inhabited a body on the adventure of life, trying to find my way. There was no use in taking things too seriously or in fretting over what it was all about; the destination was the journey.

I understood that being comfortable in my own mind was the first step in attaining peace and giving me the potential for success, but also that it was not a one-and-done process. My ultimate goal was self-love, but I knew that attaining that goal would not always be so simple. If I could befriend myself, then I could deal with anything the future held.

My mom texted me on the tail end of these realizations, asking me out to dinner. Even though I was on a psychedelic drug, it sounded lovely, so I collected myself and got in the car with her. For the first time in as long as I could remember, I felt comfortable in my head, and this gave me strength and confidence. When we made it to the restaurant, I did not worry about the opinions of others or how I appeared. I loved myself, and when we were brought to our table, it was as if I were my own pleasant company, in addition to my mother. To add even more profundity to the evening, when I thanked the waiter for water, I was told I had good manners. But of course, I'm on psilocybin mushrooms; who's the wiser?

Our dinner was delightful. We feasted on soup, salad, and pasta, and then a warm apple crostata for dessert. I felt great gratitude for the opportunity to share this time with my mother and chose to save the memory as a warm picture of life's simple blessings. When the waiter brought out the check, we were in no hurry to leave, but it reminded me that our evening was ending soon. This made me melancholy at first, as I always seemed to attach myself to the moment and resist its end, but when I considered the alternative—staying here all night—the beauty of impermanence seemed to reveal itself. The end was simply another beginning, and with the hope for more good times to come, our dinner's bittersweet ending became more palatable.

Once we made it back home, I said goodbye to my mother and went upstairs to my apartment for the night. Again, I felt a bit unsettled and anxious, but I refused to give in to these feelings. I figured I just needed something to occupy my mind, so I went to my bookshelf and mulled over all the titles. The Art of War, The Doors of Perception, Fear and Loathing in Las Vegas—none of them sounded all that pleasant right now. Instead, I picked up the Bible and started reading Proverbs. I was immediately enthralled by its poetry, and my heart was settled by the affirming words of love. With each paragraph, I was soothed more, and sat there for over an hour reading the entire book. I could not remember the last time I had opened the Bible, and now it was revealing to me that I was not alone in my struggle, and that I had the constant love and company of God.

I felt a bit shy because it had been a long time since I had purposely been in God's company, but I knew that I had made a step in the right direction. My uneasiness was still present, but I had developed a kind of psychological bedrock now. I knew I was loved by the creator, so there was no need for extreme conclusions or self criticism. The way forward was with God, and though the implications of that path were yet to be realized, it was the only way to go.

My only real fear was of repeating my past, that is, drawing conclusions without following up on them. Partnering with God, loving myself, and going forward with grace were all serving me wonderfully, but would they last? Would I wake up again tomorrow and go right back to my old ways, or would I take my experience to heart and truly make a change? My history pointed towards a couple weeks of apparent transformation before descending right back into apathy and addiction, but I was hopeful this time. And, even if I were to fall back, the point of this trip was not to lock myself into a set of behaviors and then get upset if I faltered, but rather to take each day for its own beauty.

Chapter 10

Paranoia

I did not know how addictive it would be to contemplate my assailant's plan over and over, nor that LSD would plant the seed of that addiction, or that marijuana would fertilize it. For over two years, my mind churned with thoughts of how Louis was going to kill me. This mindset damaged my relationships, caused my spiritual faith to deteriorate, decreased my trust in others, hardened my heart, and ultimately changed who I am. I consider the change for the better. I would not go back to where I was before.

Coming up on the other side of paranoia, however, required an incredible amount of suffering, crescendoed by a full-on mental break. Before going there, though, the former patterns must be laid so that the subsequent fate completes the picture. What follows is an imperfect chronicle of two years of volatile suspicion, self-doubt, panicked change, relational strife, and radical perceptual shifts.

***

The depths of paranoia contain great illusions and fictitious paths to safety that are as convincing as reality. Sinister plots appear out of nowhere. Doom seems to hide behind every corner, yet when it does not come to, it leaves behind evidence. The words of others, heard previously as innocent, become malicious and ominous. Death itself is not the greatest foe, but rather the one who brings it and finds great pleasure in doing so. Thus, paranoia brings you into the mind of the insane and shows the reasons for your end. You build walls to defend the shameful parts of yourself so that no one will find reason to harm you. You try to share little of your successes and happiness so that evil has less of a grave to gloat on.

Time goes by. Nothing happens, but evil torments you. It plots against you and makes you ask: Am I prepared enough? I walk through times of joy, but evil is always there haunting me. It whispers, "You do not deserve this joy. I will steal it from you." I can never fully relax, for that is when evil will strike. I try to predict the setting of the attack so I am prepared. Through the eyes of evil, I see my own fears and the torture I would find most agonizing. It matters not where I go—evil is inescapable. I believe that every step I take is seen, though I try to cover my tracks. My days are filled with omens as evil lusts over the things I love.

My soul hardens as all that I cherish is threatened before my eyes. I can only do so much to ensure my safety, but the daily barrage of fear arms me to the teeth. True delusion fills my mind as I recognize my futility and appeal to the unseen. I abstain from pleasures, from indulgence and rest. Death surely shall not fall on a good and industrious person.

The wonder of what life for my enemies and loved ones will be like once I am gone is disturbingly captivating. Pain, inflicted on those I love—this is another satisfying piece of my murderer's meal. More days of my life had always seemed to be on the horizon, but now they are plotted against. What terrible wrong had I done to deserve this? None—it was simply my character and blessings that evil would seek to destroy.

To the people around me, I ask questions carefully, so as not to alert them to my dark mental state. I desire as much information as possible, along with a sane person's perspective. I want to know if the patterns I am seeing are cause for alarm, or sheer coincidence. Does anyone share my concern, or do I stand alone in my suspicion? As convincing as others' answers are, they do not change my perspective. I know that evil is coming for me.

***

The first time after that acid trip with Louis when I began to genuinely wonder if he still had malicious intent was when he and Oz came over for a smoke session. This was a few months after the trip, and a pretty standard occasion. They would drive to my apartment in the evening, we would do some dabs and zone out, and then they would leave a few hours later. This is exactly what happened that night, but right before they were about to leave, Louis started telling us about a documentary he had watched. Supposedly, according to this show, if someone was killed on federal land, the murderer could not be tried. A trial would have to include a jury of their peers, but because the death occurred on federal land, and there were no people technically residing in that area, there could be no jury.

I figured this had to be false, and voiced my disbelief, but then Oz chimed in with support for the idea. I still did not believe them, but the way they looked at me made me feel like they were thinking, "he's just in denial about this loophole in the law." I refused to buy into it, especially while stoned out of my mind, but I wondered why Louis had watched the documentary, and why he chose to bring it up now. Then they left, leaving me to chew on this idea with my high brain at 11 pm.

That familiar old feeling of paranoia came back as I put myself into the mind of my murderer. The only reason Louis would tell me this was to invoke fear and make me consider the possibility that he would get away with murder. I did not see an alternative—there was no other good reason why he had shared this with me, unless he was on some "mission" to fix loopholes in the legal system. Oz's support for the idea was also frightening; the two of them lived together, and I could only imagine the conversations they had when I was not around.

This pretty much affirmed my decision to never go to a remote location with Louis, but sure enough, in the weeks following, camping was all he could talk about. This was not necessarily unusual, given that he was an outdoorsy person, but now this documentary was the only thing that came to my mind when he talked about going on hikes. I was also reminded of that moment in the woods on our acid bike ride when I had distrusted him and his intent. Nothing had come of that, but I had not forgotten that feeling.

Shortly after I was told about this supposed "murderer loophole" in the law, Louis and Oz told me another story. This time, it was about one of our old classmates. Her brother had been involved in the fatal shooting of a drug dealer. The story was that he and his friend were planning to rob the dealer, so they set up a fake deal in a parking lot and pulled a gun. When the dealer tried to escape, they shot him in the head. I could not get the image of a gruesomely stained back seat in a 90s sedan out of my head. Not only did these kids feel the need to get a gun and rob someone, but the whole deal had been over weed. Three lives ruined and many more affected.

I wondered which parking lot it happened in, and painted a picture of the scene in my mind. I could only imagine the expression of shock on the robber's face after he pulled the trigger, and I felt even more dread at the notion of the rest of his life being spent in a concrete cell. I shared my disgust with Louis and Oz, but in the back of my mind, I was comparing this event to previous disturbing experiences with Louis. I had not forgotten Halloween night 2016, with the stories of hitman gangs and vicious assault, nor had I forgotten our harrowing trip to the beach with weed edibles. I also had not forgotten the fear brought on by his maniacal laughing on my first DMT trip.

These thoughts and feelings were convincing, like pieces of a puzzle. I chose to entertain them, so little by little, everything began to fit the homicidal narrative. I continued having a relationship with Louis and sincerely tried to dismiss these feelings, but the dread and paranoia always came back. I would regularly think through the things that he had said and done, and decide which ones were meant to deceive or trap me. I had to be wise to his game, but revealing my suspicions would not only make him and others think I was crazy, it would also reveal that I was aware of his intentions. I wanted to be wrong about him, but the distrust had been chiseled into my mind over many months of undisciplined thought, chronic cannabis use, partial psychosis, and a blinding hatred for evil.

I did not realize the impact these paranoid thoughts were having on me, or just how accepting I had become of them. Instead of questioning the idea that my friend wanted to kill me, I just decided that it was a fact. I had to prepare myself for any attempt on my life, and certainly avoid going to any remote places with him, but part of my motive was to prove myself right. If my suspicions were true, then my feelings would have a basis in reality, and then theoretically, this game we were in would be over. That's what I really wanted—for the whole thing to be over. I was so sick of worrying about getting killed. I was done looking behind my back, trying to read signs and living in fear. The more compelling evidence I found to support my suspicions, the closer I was to putting them behind me.

Had I been so fortunate to receive the gifts of doubt and recognition of my own delusions, perhaps I could have come out of my paranoia sooner. The problem was that it was a life or death situation, so it seemed incredibly foolish to dismiss all that I was seeing. I refused to stop looking for Louis's sinister plot because finding it would either help me stay alive, or find a bit of evidence to prove myself right and end the whole thing. Some days seemed to show more evidence than others, but I had no doubt that Louis was out to get me.

This fear permeated all facets of our relationship. I chose to be strategically withdrawn, while trying to appear relaxed. I was very careful about what I shared, and I tried to make myself seem as if I were unhappy because I felt that Louis's desire to destroy my happiness was his motive for killing me. I did not talk about my successes or joys unless he shared his as well. I tried to make myself seem as unrewarding of a kill as possible, but everything, even the basic functions of life, seemed to bother him. I could not drink water without feeling like I was doing so undeservingly. I could not even love myself.

Marijuana was a huge amplifying factor of my paranoia, and I have no doubt that if I had quit smoking, I would have found peace much sooner. I did not differentiate between high thoughts and sober logic, so all my thoughts blended together as one mass of distorted perception. Weed held too much influence over my thoughts, and instead of being skeptical of the ideas it proposed, I went along with them. Drugs also undeniably impacted my thinking even while I wasn't high, so the whole problem just compounded and resulted in my feelings of constant turbulence. I knew that my psyche was unstable, but I considered it normal for someone facing a murderer, and I used my brief periods of sobriety and peace to tell myself that I was not crazy.

About a year after the trip, I began to fear others as well, and I started to think that Louis was not the only one out to get me. Bo sent me the song "Magic Wand" by Tyler the Creator, which talks about getting a gun and killing an opposing lover, and I even suspected that Dakota had ill intent after piecing together strange things that he had said. I was threatened from many sides, so I planned each day to avoid danger. I kept an erratic schedule so no one could trace me. I considered the locations where I was the most vulnerable and plotted courses of action for whatever came my way. I did not have a gun, so I had to get creative with my self-defense.

I began appealing to the divine more often as time went on, and I took actions that I thought would make the Creator keep me safe. I practiced charity, kindness, and compassion for strangers. I read the Bible on and off, periodically went to church, and tasked myself with things that would make me appear industrious and helpful. Regardless of how self-assured I was, though, my relapses into fear were infrequent but guaranteed. I enjoyed psychological stability for months sometimes, only to have one marijuana experience spin the reel of murder before my eyes once again and bring me to the same conclusion: that Louis was out to kill me and that my time of perceived security had been an illusion.

I did not share the full extent of these ideas with anyone, but I did tell my girlfriend quite a bit. She acted with love and agreed with my skepticism, but my own wavering made it difficult for her to give me advice. She maintained that Louis's actions were odd and that my feelings were somewhat justified, but she failed to understand why I continued spending time with him. I did not understand it either. I experienced radical ideological swings between feeling friendship with Louis and vehement distrust of him. This, combined with my general self-doubt, created a great deal of irregularity in the philosophies that I shared with her. One thing that was absolutely certain, though, was that I loved her, she loved me, and any attempt to sabotage that would be met with fierce hostility.

Time, bad luck, and even more bad decisions caused my paranoia to grow. I began looking into old murder cases, trying to understand motives, methods, and warning signs. I applied my own experiences to past victims, looking for mistakes they had made, signs they had missed, and traps that had been laid for them. I considered that my murder could be made to look like an accident while still inflicting a horrifying degree of torture upon me. I explored what I hated most through the mind of someone who wanted to kill me and wondered if I had ever revealed my true worst nightmares to Louis. I considered what my girlfriend's life would be like without me, and pictured how my killer would swoon her into his arms and bask in his disgustingly indulgent victory. There was quite literally nothing worse—I get tortured to death, my killer gets away with it, and then gets all my blessings.

Truly, these were things I had never thought about before. I did not believe in or accept humans' great capability for evil, so I campaigned against it. To me, Louis was the representation of evil. I found this idea even more convincing when I went to his and Oz's house one evening. They had a roommate who liked to horror movies, and this fit my narrative even more closely. I pictured the lot of them excitedly sitting on the couch enjoying human carnage and massacre. Hatred for all things in that dimension seared me inside like an inferno.

I believed that I was bringing myself closer to good. The reality was that evil was having its intended blinding effect on me. My mind had become what I despised, and life was bleak because of it. Every corner had pain waiting behind it, and every person had ulterior motives. My moments of happiness were perpetually haunted by the looming threat of their destruction, and so fear guided me. I did not long for the past because it too held fear. I could see no alternative to what was. I was living on borrowed time, and I could not escape that feeling, even while looking into my dearest love's eyes. My heart burned with passion and frighteningly intense love, yet evil whispered in my ear that it would all be gone soon.

Years of this weathered me like a stone in the middle of a desert. I learned to live with paranoia and the constant threat of what I loved being stolen. I knew that there was only so much I could do to prevent my demise, and while I built walls and burned bridges, I continued to live my life. I spent lots of time loving my girlfriend and enjoying what I thought could be our last times together. I grew closer to my mother and family. I sorted my documents, cleaned my apartment, and made sure that my important writing and other things would be available to my loved ones.

As wearing as this was on my heart, I couldn't help but compare my current situation to the way things used to be. The old worries of when I would move out, how my relationship with my girlfriend would change when she came home from college, what it might be like to live without my parents, how I would deal with injuries as I got old, what I would do after college, and if I would ever formally share my writing: these were all were small by comparison. Now I did not even know if I would live to see the next day. This was poetically exemplified by my old cat—I had thought that she would die 4 years ago, yet here she was, healthy and happy. I had never considered the possibility I might die before she did; that I might never come home to her.

Bad luck came for me in the summer of 2019. My city was in the midst of an extremely violent year, and hearing gunshots and sirens while I was high at 2 am became a regular occurrence. Loud pops followed by the roar of distant fleeing motors made my entire torso tense and traumatically stilled my high brain. It was a stark contrast: one moment I would be eating food and enjoying the intoxicating effect of a documentary on my buzzing mind: the next, sounds of destruction and sirens wrenched heart to rigidity. Then, thoughts of what kind of anguish the poor soul who had just been filled with searing lead was feeling percolated in my mind. Someone was actively dying by the hand of another, and here I was, sitting in bed high and eating snacks.

I preferred not to call the cops on these occasions because I had no desire to give a report in the middle of the night in my front yard, high and already paranoid. I felt disturbed with a sense of futility about this violence, but now the sound of fireworks and gunshots were so commonplace and intermingled that I accepted it as a reality of living in a city. These shootings did not happen without repercussions, though, and I kept my eye on the media. Most of the shootings were gang related, but one incident that stuck out to me was about a guy who had been shot on the Fourth of July in front of his girlfriend. I put myself in his place, wondering what he had done to deserve this and what it was like to lie there, helpless and dying in front of his girlfriend, knowing that he had been killed on purpose. I imagined what kind of sinister plot and resentment the killer had mulled over in his mind before shooting him, and figured that someone had the very same plans for me.

One night in particular during this summer, I was very stoned and just about to fall asleep when I heard the chilling clap of gunshots. It jolted me awake, and after only a minute, I heard my mom's dog barking aggressively downstairs. The clock said 4 am and I wondered what the hell was going on. There were sounds coming from downstairs, like slamming doors and banging, and I thought something terrible was happening. I went to my kitchen window to look into the backyard to see what the dog was barking at, but she now was standing perfectly still, frozen in place like a statue The only time I had seen her like this was when she was stalking a squirrel, pointing directly at what she was after. I looked in the direction she was facing, and just on the other side of the chain link fence stood a stocky, white-faced man holding a rifle.

    I dropped to the floor and called 9-1-1. I panickedly told them there was someone with a gun in the backyard and gave them my address. I told them I heard many gunshots, like some kind of war was raging in the background. I asked what I should do and they told me to stay put. Moments later, flashlight beams began bouncing through my backyard. I watched anxiously from the window, wondering if I would hear a shootout, but then I remembered the acid I had in the freezer. If the police were to search the house and find it, the whole call might seem like a hallucination, so I shot up and opened the freezer. One of the officers in the yard turned his head towards my window, and I knew that he saw me. The 9-1-1 operator told me to stay put, but I grabbed the tabs and returned to my hiding spot.

    Approximately two minutes had passed since my sighting of the man with the gun, and I was extremely fidgety, fearful of what would come next. I knew that I would have to talk to the police, and I thought it was a real possibility that they would come into my apartment, so I scurried to the bathroom and dropped the tabs in the toilet. I said a confident goodbye and flushed them to oblivion. Then I went back into hiding before I heard my doorbell ring. I had to go face the consequences of my actions.

I walked down the stairs slowly, preparing as best I could to face an officer in my pajamas at 4 am, high, after just reporting a gun-wielding man and gunshots. I opened my squeaky door and stepped out onto the patio. A dozen policemen, all wielding AR's and heavy gear were staring at me. I was standing two feet above all of them too, like some kind of king that had declared the need for protection. The extreme embarrassment I felt was unbearable, but I did not doubt what I had seen. The first officer questioned me, and I told him—stocky man, brown hair, white face, holding a rifle. I saw the dog pointing at him, and called. Gunshots woke me up, and I went to the window when I heard the barking and banging downstairs.

A few officers were taking notes, but when I mentioned that I was half asleep, they paused and looked up at me. I immediately began doubting my word choice and appearance. There was a long silence.

"Have you…uhhh, by any chance, been smoking anything?"

"What? I was asleep. Maybe I could have been seeing things, but I don't think so. I'm sure I saw a guy holding a rifle. I was scared."

There was another long pause, and the officers taking notes looked at each other. I knew there was some suspicion, so I tried to make myself look and sound as sober as possible. I knew that it would be unprofessional for them to keep pressuring me on this, especially given what I had just gone through, and so the interaction actually wrapped up quite quickly. Most of the cops marched away, while a couple stuck around and took down my information. I thanked them profusely for the response, and felt genuinely cared for by these people. Then my mom came out and defused the situation even more, and shortly after, they were gone.

I told my mom everything that had led up to this situation, but her version of events was scary in a different way. She thought that she had seen people in the driveway, so she stuck her head out to a bunch of cops holding AR rifles pointed toward her. This story filled me with both dread and thanks, as I could only imagine what a jumpy cop might have done. I tried to push these thoughts away and hugged my mom as I told her how scared I was. She did not question or criticize my fear, but supported me and made me feel like I was not crazy. I did not doubt what I had seen, nor did I feel that calling 911 was the wrong choice. I definitely saw the dog pointing at a guy in the yard who appeared to be holding a rifle. And, who looked strangely similar to Louis.

Chapter 11

The Secret Face

The degeneration of my relationship with Louis and Oz was caused in part by my own paranoia. However, our trio was trending towards downfall for other reasons. We had been doing the same thing for over two years now: smoking weed in my apartment and sitting around. This was awesome at first, exploring deep into the cannabis haze and reckless intoxication, but it eventually became stale. We lacked engaging conversation and creative energy. Often, the two of them were coming off a long day at work, while I was interested in going on night walks and engaging in challenging philosophical discussions. We were on different wavelengths.

The breakdown of our relationship was not all my fault. Louis was very critical of my ideas, and Oz seemed to blindly support him. I became overly defensive around the two of them because my smallest mistakes were made fun of, and I often suspected that they were not fully truthful with me. I had no doubt that they were talking behind my back, and I picked up on this awkward vibe more and more as time went on. I had been through a lot with these two guys, and I was used to being an open book around them, so their dishonesty left me feeling vulnerable and betrayed.

Instead of engaging with me on the deeper level that I desired, the two of them seemed resistant and often responded with sarcasm. I did not feel respected. They did not value my ideas, and often played down my successes. I began keeping track of our conversations and unspoken communications. I put up walls and stopped sharing my feelings, so our relationship digressed even further. Marijuana only amplified my feelings and caused me to withdraw entirely and approach our interactions with suspicion. Their lack of transparency, paired with my paranoia and my perceptual uncertainty caused by psychoactives, eventually caused me to take a break from the relationship.

Reflecting back on the relationship did not help matters, as I recalled many instances of awkward silence, broken eye contact, whispers, and hasty topic shifts. This all served as compelling evidence that Louis and Oz were not being fully truthful with me, so I shifted my focus to my girlfriend and myself. I worked to reassure myself and my beliefs and tried to make sense of why I was feeling so poorly about my friends. I did recognize my own role in the breakdown of our relationship, but I also could not entirely dismiss the lack of honesty and criticism that I was getting from them. I also knew that weed was playing a huge role in my paranoia, so I ended up taking a break from it too. Then, after a month of not seeing Louis and Oz, I invited them to a dinner at Outback Steakhouse.

***

On the night of our dinner, our friendship seemed semi-revamped after this time off. I was not picking up on nearly as much criticism from them, and though a bit of an awkward vibe lingered, things were looking up. The break from weed had calmed my mind, and I realized that part of the problem with our relationship was that I sought enrichment from it. Our time together was better spent relaxing and having fun, so I would do my self-fulfillment before seeing them. This put us all on the same frequency of simply getting stoned and vibing to music, and that is exactly where I was one July night. Louis and Oz came over in the evening, along with Heub, and we were all going to get high.

Because of the temporary pause I had put on our friendship, Louis and Oz were very careful with their words that night. The break was over now, as far as they knew, but the exact reason for it had not been fully revealed to them. I had doubted, criticized, and seethed about the relationship. I also had a history of subtly cutting ties with people, which was not a fair or loving practice, but I often chose it instead of forcing myself to deal with an uncomfortable situation. Despite the negativity, I wanted to preserve our relationship, and though I did not realize it at the time, the two of them did care for me. In a way, their criticisms were beneficial because they made me address uncertainties in myself that I had not considered.

That threatening vibe seemed absent on this night. I was not up in my head about what they were thinking or especially doubtful of my own philosophies. We were just together as friends, enjoying a night of smoking and relaxation for the sole purpose of fun. I was comfortable, even when Heub joined the dynamic an hour later. He was late as usual, but I eventually got a phone call from him, and before I answered, he had opened the door and was coming upstairs. I liked this; he was comfortable enough to let himself in. He joined us in the living room and started talking about his job packing lotion at a factory. I sat back and enjoyed the company, participating casually in conversation and feeling a great sense of peace. We were all buddies again, enjoying a low-pressure situation. I loved it, and daydreamed about future travels and smoke sessions with these guys.

  I brought out the weed a little while after Heub got settled, and after passing around a bong, I decided to pack up the vaporizer. This was the first time in a while that I had gotten high, but the vibe was positive and I wanted to lift it higher. I also had quite a bit of kief in my grinder, so I packed it into a fat bowl in my vape. Just before starting it up, Oz cautioned me, "Christian, don't you think you should go slow with it?"

  I was already stoned when he said this, so the words just bounced off me, but then I asked, "Why?"

  "It's your first time smoking in like a month, isn't it? Let's just smoke some bud."

  I shook my head; I was not even a little worried. I had taken multiple tolerance breaks over the past couple years and never paced myself getting back into weed. Sure, it was a fat kief bowl, but it was also in a mellow vaporizer that would be passed around to four people. I did not heed Oz's advice and took some long puffs before passing it. The vapor was potent but arid, like a gale from the Sonoran Desert mixed with a robust pine resin. There was still a hint of sweetness, though, stimulating saliva and catching my rear taste buds like a crisp soda.

Only a few minutes had passed before I came up with a brilliant idea: Balderdash! This was a board game with a deck of cards. Each card had five words on it, one from each of these categories: famous person, movie, acronym, law, and word, along with their definitions. The dasher selects a word and reads it aloud, while the rest of the group writes on a piece of paper what they think that word means. However, then the dasher seamlessly blends and reads aloud everyone's answers along with the correct answer, and players then have to guess which one is correct. Players win points by answering correctly. Deception comes into play because players also win points if another player guesses their answer, so even if a player does not know the answer, if they write something convincing to the group, they still win points.

After nearly an hour of trying to explain this game to my high friends, we got into it and had a blast. Our answers were wacky and creative, and no matter how serious we tried to be, laughter filled the room. The contrast between the intensity of our careful reading of the cards and the absurdity of our answers made the game even funnier, as if we were potheads putting on a performance in court.

"Serious" things are hilarious when you're high because everything seems so trivial, yet we were able to keep the game going and trick each other at every turn.

One of the most fun rounds was with the word "glossarium." I was the one reading the card, but Heub submitted an answer that I could not quite make out. If I was not able to smoothly read his answer, it would give away that it was not the correct one, so Heub and I stepped into the other room and he whispered into my ear, "a section… of a book…used for references." I had to contain my laughter, and then I asked him to repeat it once more so that I was sure I had it right. "A section of a book used for references." I rehearsed this over and over in my head, all the while knowing he was thinking of a GLOSSARY. Then we reentered the living room, and I read aloud all the answers. Sure enough, Louis guessed Heub's; our backroom deal had worked. The right definition had something to do with plants, and I was proud of my seamless integration.

The game kept moving, and with everyone enjoying themselves, I was happier than I had been in a long time with this group. The game was creative and immersive, which was a stark contrast to the past year of dull intoxication. I had plenty more board games, too, and wondered why I had not thought of them sooner. Even a simple card game while high would lift everybody's mental state, and I got excited at the thought of getting together one day to make our own game. Exercises in probability and strategy were easy to come up with when we were high, and I knew that by using our combined creativity, we had the potential to make something awesome.

I realized that I was quite stoned when I was trying to read out the answers, and while struggling to make out Louis's, Oz said, "Yeah, you can read mine. I wrote it clearly."

I immediately felt like a teacher in an elementary classroom. "Yes, very good, Oz," I said facetiously, folding my hands. I then looked at Louis pretending that glasses were resting on the bridge of my nose. His face was pink, and then he threw up his hands, complaining about the shitty colored pencil I had given him.

"Hmph," I remarked pompously, looking at Oz's equally dull red-colored pencil. The whole thing was inescapably hilarious. Heub did not quite seem to get it, as he was staring into space, but that was typical of him. I was surprised that he was even coherent enough to play the game, as he had a history of passing out from just a little weed. That said, passing out was not particularly unusual for any of us. I could not count the number of times I had been told that my carpet was comfy, and had verified that fact plenty of times myself. This was a safe place to do it, though; we didn't mess with each other while we were sleeping, and I always encouraged people to stay the night instead of driving home high. The sleeping arrangements weren't great, consisting of the couch and the floor, but at the very least my apartment was warm and you didn't have to worry about anybody giving you a hard time.

We were about a dozen rounds in when it was my turn to be the dasher again. I pulled a card and selected a movie called "The Secret Face." Everyone had to write what they thought it was about, and I chose that movie because I knew they would never guess that it was about photographer who takes pictures of people in Istanbul.

"Okay, it's a movie this time. 'The Secret Face,' I said mysteriously. Pencils jotting on paper were the only sounds in the room as I hoped to trick all of my friends. One by one, they handed me their answers, and then I carefully read each one.

A man who hides a second life from his wife. – From Louis.

About a young girl wearing a mask hoping to please…something. – From Oz.

It's about the unseen branch of the U.S. government that manipulates currency. – From Heub.

My heart rate rose and my chest felt tight. I stared at the cards and rehearsed them in my mind. Then I started reading them aloud. "A man who hides a second face from his wife." My voice shook, and then I moved to Oz's. "About a young girl wearing a mask trying to please… something." I stopped. I couldn't make out what he had written. I looked directly at Oz with a feeling of shame. Then onto Heub's: "An unseen branch of the U.S. government that manipulates currency." I shuffled the answers and then read the real answer. Complete silence followed.

"Could you read them again?" Louis asked.

The tightness in my chest increased—Why did he want me to reread them? So that I would suffer through these accusations once again? I did it anyway, all over again. The silence continued, and my stomach burned. My whole body felt like it was about to quiver, and my breath came in short gasps. These were in fact accusations. I was the man hiding a face from his girlfriend, she was wearing a mask and trying to please something wretched that was me, and Heub knew that I had money. And the other answer—a photographer who takes pictures of people in Istanbul—that was who I really was, a lowlife that makes pornography.

I leaned over, putting my elbows onto my knees. I stared at the ground and said: "Louis, why do you want to harm me?" My thoughts had just manifested into words. I could not hold them back any more. Now I was going to see their consequences.

"What are you talking about?" Louis said, astonished. Heub and Oz stared at me.

"I...I feel like you want to hurt me."

"Is this about that acid trip, Christian?" Heub asked jokingly. I thought for a moment, and answered no. It was not. It had gone beyond that.

"Just pick another card," Louis suggested. I paused for a moment and then fished one out. The first thing I saw was: "a shoulder surgeon in Thailand." I had experienced shoulder problems since high school; of course, this was the card. It was a "blameless" way to off me.

"It feels like you want to kill me," I said with sorrow.

"What?!" Louis exclaimed.

"Hold up! You really think Louis is trying to kill you? I live with him. Look at him. He's not trying to kill anybody," Oz interjected. I lifted my eyes to see Louis's disturbed expression, but then I remembered that moment in the kitchen when we were on acid. He had tricked my mom into thinking that he was innocent. This was another act. Of course he would respond this way to these accusations.

The answers spun round and round in my head—a man lying to his wife, a girl trying to please something, hidden money, a lowlife photographer. They morphed and changed—a movie about a man who gets killed, a girl who is freed when her oppressive boyfriend dies, a government agency that bankrupts a sinner.

"Do you believe in God?" I asked, looking at Louis.

"Yes, I do," he answered, seeming unshaken by the question.

"Do you believe God works through people?" I asked, without listening to the answer. He said something about deism, but the question was for myself. I did believe that God worked through people, and that Louis was the one he would work through. I had taken my life for granted. My blessings, my girlfriend, and my time. I did not deserve any of it, so it would all be taken from me by God. He would work through Louis to kill me because I was the one hiding a face, my girlfriend was the one with Stockholm syndrome, and my money would be taken by the government.

Then I heard the door open. Was someone else here to finish me off?

"Christian?" my mom hollered, walking up the stairs. I did not say anything. Then she entered the living room, where we sat in silence.

"What's going on?"

"Louis wants to kill me," I said with depressed certainty. My friends scoffed at the absurdity, but my mom rushed to calm me down.

"No, he doesn't. You guys are just up here partying. Nobody's trying to hurt you."

"I wish you were right," I said with sadness.

"Dude, your buddy Louis is not trying to kill you. He's your friend. He cares about you." My mom explained.

I stared at the ground and spun the things my friends had written round and round in my mind. This could not be a coincidence. Those answers were sinisterly calculated to expose my sins and pierce my heart.

"Look what they wrote. The cards, here!" I said to my mom, pushing the papers towards her. She eyeballed them and remained unphased.

"Have you had any water? Why don't you get a drink or something?"

This was a good idea, so I left the room and went to the kitchen, where four water bottles lay scattered on the countertop. Why did I have so many? Why had I bought them? Fear: I was afraid of not having water. What did my friends think of this? I didn't deserve this many, and they wouldn't do me any good dead. Water could help me, though, so I filled up a bottle and took a big swig. Then my mouth tingled and it felt like coffee grounds in my throat. I inspected the bottle, but the water was clear. I had been drugged—my friends had put something in my bottle! I couldn't tell them this—it would make me seem even more crazy.

I returned to the living room, where my mom was trying to explain to my friends what was going on. On the black couch, Louis and Oz sat in darkness, while I sat next to Heub, illuminated by the bright white light of the hallway. I saw Heub differently in this moment: he was an ally. Louis and Oz were the ones criticizing and threatening me, not him. I considered Heub's family: His conservative parents, regular attendance at church, and strong value system. For years, I had wondered what the point of all that was, being so conventional and upstanding. Now I got it. Safety and faith, that's what they were about. The world of drugs and darkness brought death and suffering, but the path of family, light, and morality brought life and prosperity.

I was on the boundary between these two worlds with a choice before me. Would I pick the path of the blissful abyss or commit to working hard for a family, house, and prosperous life? My foot had been in the door of both worlds for years, but my recent actions were pulling me further into the void. There was no middle way—I had to make a choice. I could not have a life with my dearest love if a part of me remained in this other world. Regardless of which way I chose, I knew I would have to make a tremendous sacrifice, but at this moment, I realized that more important to me than anything else was life with her. Never before had it been "put up for grabs" in this way, but now everything made sense to me. A "friend" who is close to me sees me taking my blessings for granted and seizes the opportunity to kill them.

I didn't regard Louis as a person, but instead as a prophet. While my mom was directing the conversation, he said I was his best friend, and this struck me down. I only considered for a second what I meant to him before once again falling back into the idea of his deception. This was yet another trick. Everything with him was a vortex twisting towards my murder. Everything happening was fate, and it was up to me to decide how things would go forward.

My mom pleaded with me to regain my sanity, and while the belief that I had been drugged and betrayed stayed firmly in my mind, I fought to normalize my actions. Louis had been brought to tears by my ruthless accusations, while the others remained confused and disturbed. There was no way out of this situation while I continued my manic speech, so I verbally agreed with my mom. She eventually got Louis and me to hug, which momentarily broke me before I returned to my paranoia. It all felt like some kind of sick joke. I had to play dumb and act like my intuition and instincts were wrong, all the while knowing I would one day be vindicated.

    I sat in my chair, staring at the ground and spinning the cards over and over in my head. Everyone in that room knew that I was still unwell. My body felt weak and exposed, and I could almost see myself from the perspective of another, ashamed and afraid. I could not take back the things I had said. My paranoia about Louis had boiled over, and with a heavy heart, I now sat like a husk. I sincerely believed that I was destined for a tortuous death at Louis's hand, and this feeling remained as all my friends anxiously packed up and left. The last glimpse of hope was right before Louis left—he looked at me with eyes of worry, and, for a second, I felt his compassion and genuine concern for me. My distrust of him momentarily dissolved, and for one moment, I saw our broken relationship as a casualty of my own foolishness.

    My delusions lasted for the next two days, convincing me that Louis and Oz had in fact drugged me. It did not matter anymore, though. Whether my distrust of them was as small as suspecting gossip behind my back, or as large as plotting to murder me, they had betrayed me. I had confided vulnerable parts of myself to them, and their dishonesty violated my trust and irreparably broke our relationship. It was my own fault for revealing so much of my self and expecting them to revere it, and theirs for not recognizing how much they meant to me.

Chapter 12

Chasing The Ocean Sky

Three years later, my penitence and wistfulness are not over, but better chronicled and understood. There are things that can never be changed, scars that will always show, and memories that remain enigmatic. Reckless and curious were these times, speckled with dread, love, magic, pain and madness. Swift in nature and entrapping like a swirling vortex, these happenings only start to make sense after the fact. Undeniable is the duality of their impacts, changing the way that I see the world forever. Like a peek into the heavens or a voyage into darkness, these experiences were unforgettable. My goal is not to suppress the difficult parts of them, or long for the lovely ones, but to go forward with an idealistic perspective.

That night was the last I saw of Oz, and though I got together with Louis a few times after, our relationship had been destroyed. We both tried to make things work, and though I got over my fear of him killing me, the scars of the past proved too haunting. This night was also the last time I smoked marijuana, and my sobriety caused a radical shift in my habits and friendships. The first year brought the most perceptual and behavioral changes, but I was careful not to attribute all of them to my sobriety. The benefits were unmistakable, but I also knew that some of these changes were natural and a part of learning with time.

My progress towards clarity and peace came slowly, but monthly milestones and reflection powerfully affirmed my choice of sobriety. One of the pieces that I underestimated most was marijuana's role in my friendships. Stopping smoking resulted in me spending less time with people, and it simply ended some relationships. I tried not to linger on this too much, and gave my old friends the benefit of the doubt, but the truth of the matter was that weed was the only thing that held some of my relationships together. This realization came with an edge, but it made me cherish my lasting friendships that much more. I also recognized that it was natural for people to come in out of your life. Weed had a unifying effect on people, and with me being an introvert all my life, this plant caused me to meet dozens of people outside of school that I would otherwise have never known.

I would be a liar if I said I do not miss marijuana, and a fool to write myself off psychedelics for the rest of my life. That said, I am abstaining now, and know that I still have years of growth and learning to undergo before even considering stepping back in. Sobriety has proven to be fun and empowering, and I am now able to do previously unthinkable things with clarity and confidence. Most importantly, I have found stability and take pride in knowing that my sobriety enables me to handle the majority of life's challenges. I am not so bold as to claim that I can face everything with unwavering resolve, but I do know that, under most circumstances, I have the lucidity to act with logic, grace, and love. This was a large motivating factor—that, no matter the hour of the day, I am able to drive to help a loved one, be emotionally supportive, and have the ability to protect everything that I love. Psychedelics did not allow me to do that.

I have come out on the other side of substance exploration with the same conclusion I went in with: People have a right to use substances, and it is absurd to jail them for it. Some feel empowered with their use, while others are terrified and destroyed, but denial of that choice is fundamentally inconsistent with bodily autonomy and personal liberty. The notion of government bodies "protecting" people from hard drugs is a flat out lie, evidenced by the legality of cigarettes and alcohol. A much more compelling factor is money. Big Pharma's billion dollar a year industry, criminal syndicates making billions from the illegal drug trade, giant prisons surviving off of locking people away for drug crimes. many psychoactive plants only becoming legal once they are taxed, regulated, and controlled; the reasons why the drug war continues are crystal clear.

When I was first introduced to psychedelics and learned about the drug war, I had high hopes for reform and cultural change. The data seemed so clear on the ineffectiveness of prohibition, and with the growing medical research into psychedelics, I thought it would only be a matter of time before they were made legal. At first, it seemed like a conspiracy, but with more time and research, I realized that these plant medicines were being purposely restricted by our ruling bodies. Keeping drugs illegal makes lots of people lots of money. You can believe that the government made certain substances illegal to keep its citizens safe, but the amount of violence, destroyed families, ruined lives, and bloodshed as a direct consequence of the drug policies begs to differ.

I was still early on in my exploration when I realized how deplorable the situation was for psychonauts. I wanted to make a change, though. Psychedelic research and exploration were an intense passion of mine, and so I invested a great deal of myself into them. I had a hard time explaining to people what exactly it was that I was doing, but I remained confident in my mission of helping others. My experiences with these substances also only heightened my curiosity, and with so much personal freedom and naivety, I saw no reason to stop exploring.

Traditional hallucinogens played a big role in producing my psychosis, but I believe that weed was the biggest factor. Some have claimed that marijuana is never the same after psychedelics, but with my first mushroom experience so close to the first time I smoked weed, I did not have a good gauge for what a "baseline" high was like. I had not started experimenting with psychoactives looking for inebriating bliss, but rather with a curiosity and yearning for divine effects. I wanted sacred knowledge and strategies for bettering my life, so I became extremely gullible and swayed by my experiences. Weed did this very well. It made everything feel fated and laden with messages from the universe. This is ultimately what I decided that psychosis was: the overexaggerated idea that everything happens for a reason, and that people can somehow perceive and control their fate.

This realization came more than a year before I quit smoking weed. I believed in predestination which ultimately caused a war in my mind between the polarized ideas of destiny versus free will, so I kept returning to the conclusion of the acid trip where I thought everybody was a robot. The idea of inescapable fate was just that—everything was a system. That trip brought me to the furthest degree of that notion, and I knew for sure that going down that path was maddening. Marijuana seemed to exaggerate those ideas though, so in order for me to have a pleasant experience with it, I had to exercise a great deal of mental control.

I believed that overcoming those ideas was the key to finding my peace, but a larger factor at play was the death of my naivety. I had been exposed to evil on many fronts, confronted with violence and danger in my city, and made to face my worst fears of losing my love and my life. I had been betrayed and lied to, hurt and left alone, and forced to face my hatreds, doubts, and the darkest places of my mind. Countless times, I deluded myself into panic and dread, and distorted my perceptions of my friends and family. I thought I deserved my pain and that any pleasures were fated to be grotesquely destroyed. Disastrous it was to step into the mind of my killer—doing so destroyed my self-image and caused me to believe that changing who I was was the only way to survive.

If the solution to overcoming my fear had been as simple as quitting drugs, I would have written them off and never looked back. The reality is, though, that I would not change anything. My naivety was my weakness. I was vulnerable, gullible, sensitive and overly trusting. My pursuit of psychedelia was reckless, and I am thankful for the traps of doubt, fear, uncertainty, and existential dread that I faced. I experienced great suffering and became stronger. Part of me died, and what replaced it was a tenacious, weathered, and hardened man. Through exposure to grief, hatred and horror, I developed the tools to handle them. I cannot go back to what I was, and I cannot live life resentful, so I must go forward using my pain for the better.

I have described nostalgia in this book as not only a longing for the past, but also a desire for a less broad perception of the world. I believe this to be one of the main reasons why nostalgia is such a peculiar emotion, and why trying to recreate the past is unfulfilling, even when the experience is closely replicated. The loss of the past is not always physical; places, people, and activities may remain the same, but what is missing is your awareness of that time. This can be especially true of childhood experiences, when so much lies outside of one's awareness, but the fact remains that humans' ever growing perception inevitably demystifies some facets of their experience. A clear example of this is the "what lies behind the closed door" analogy. One's imagination runs wild with thoughts of what could be behind the door, and that is what is enchanting. The second time that door is opened, however, no matter how much buildup and replication there is of the initial experience, it is impossible to capture that same feeling.

This is the reason why I do not blame drugs for the loss of my naivety; that loss was inevitable. The irony is that I used psychoactives as a way to cling to my childhood, but after all was said and done, they ended up accelerating my maturation. My exploration occurred in a highly transitional stage of my life, so there is no doubt that my choices and destination were greatly affected by psychedelics. But, I love where I am now and where I am heading, which is why I respectfully give these experiences their due. As I have grown older, I realize that great strength is only possible through suffering and perseverance, and having experienced that, the power of my past has become that much more apparent. I consider myself blessed to have had the opportunity to undergo what I did, and come out with newfound vigor.

I believe it is repression to deny the past its positive and alluring nature. Everyone experiences shades of nostalgia, and though I do grieve the loss of my naivety, I do not desire to go back to the past. Instead, that immersive feeling of curiosity about psychedelics, spirituality, and the ineffable is what I miss. Exploration of these things was exhilarating, and I had discovered so much so quickly that a sudden, choppy end was only natural. I had gone from innocent boy to full-fledged psychonaut, potential murder victim, aspiring husband and father, seasoned mental illness battler, philosopher, and fierce survivor, all in a matter of a couple years. Slowing down that train was unavoidably difficult.

The future holds untold horizons of discovery, wonder, and curiosity, so even though I long for my past, I know that novel adventures await. Psychedelics brought me that feeling of awe for a long time, and though I am not writing off their power for the future, they revealed to me many things I had to do without them. Discovery is the most alluring aspect of hallucinogens, and in that way, they connect to childhood because they rekindle the spirit of wonder. As age brings freedom and power with more work and responsibility, that adventurous spirit can dwindle, but the desire for adventure is eternal in all of us. With more to lose, the idea of venturing into the unknown is scary, but letting go is key to experiencing the cosmos. Replace the worry of losing things with thankfulness for them, and then by letting go, we gain everything, and harmonize with the universes law of nothing being lost.

An end inevitably presents itself as a double edged sword, as there is satisfaction in completion, but also a somber tone of change. It would be foolish for anyone to claim that their past has been totally digested, as memories will ferment and reveal new dimensions with time. However, chronicling memories is the greatest grasp for understanding. I know that my readers' understandings will differ and align with mine in unique ways, and that is the beauty of any story—the lessons and mysteries are not fixed. They are different for each person and evolve over time with further contemplation. Just as the act of writing these stories has brought me a greater understanding of myself and my past,

I believe wholeheartedly in their power for future understanding. So, they are indispensable not only as pictures of the past, but also as references—they are like reliable tools whose place has been earned by perseverance through the waves of existential adventure.

Now, I approach the future with zeal and a new freedom that comes from chronicling these experiences. The stories are not over; rather, they have catalyzed into a new chapter. They are foundational to my future writings and quests, and beneficial to you in ways only imaginable, so by sedulously venturing through them, we have formed an illustrious beginning.

www.ingramcontent.com/pod-product-compliance
Lightning Source LLC
Chambersburg PA
CBHW030037100526
44590CB00011B/233